*A White Lady
Doing Nothing
in the Tropics*

A White Lady Doing Nothing in the Tropics

THE STORY OF HERMAN AND MARY DIXON

Mary Dixon

Christian Publications
CAMP HILL, PENNSYLVANIA

Christian Publications
3825 Hartzdale Drive, Camp Hill, PA 17011

Faithful, biblical publishing since 1883

ISBN: 0-87509-641-7
LOC Catalog Number: 95-71782
©1996 by Christian Publications, Inc.
All rights reserved.
Printed in the United States of America

96 97 98 99 00 5 4 3 2 1

Cover portrait by Karl Foster

Unless otherwise indicated
Scripture taken from the HOLY BIBLE:
NEW INTERNATIONAL VERSION®
© 1973, 1978, 1984 by the
International Bible Society.
Used by permission of
Zondervan Publishing House.
All rights reserved.

Contents

Publisher's Note vii
Acknowledgments xv
About the Author xvii
Introduction 1
1 *Back to Borneo* 3
2 *Goodbye, America!* 9
3 *Hello, Borneo!* 20
4 *"Necessities" Versus the Kayan River* 26
5 *The Decision* 35
6 *The Apo Kayan at Last* 54
7 *Home with the People* 64
8 *Plain Living* 77
9 *A Great Chief Passes* 88
10 *A White Lady Doing Nothing in the Tropics* 99

11 Massacre at Long Nawang 108
12 "Paradise" Lost and Gained 115
13 Mission Point 124
14 Off to Conference 136
15 Shooting "Big" Rapids 155
16 Leech Trail 169
17 The Final Chapter 180
    Epilogue 189

Publisher's Note

The Jaffray Collection of Missionary Portraits was inaugurated in 1990 to chronicle the lives and ministries of Christian and Missionary Alliance missionaries. Each of the 13 books in the series which was published before this title has encompassed the entire life, to the time of writing, of the missionary or missionaries involved.

A White Lady Doing Nothing in the Tropics is a departure from the pattern. The text of this book covers only the last of three terms that Herman and Mary Dixon spent in Borneo, Indonesia. A year following their return to North America in 1952, Mary died. Herman did not return to the field.

The text also departs from the usual major emphasis on ministry. It was written as a love story, painted on a background of hardships, including almost four years in a Japanese internment camp. Any reference to the happenings of those four years in the Dixon's correspondence is negligible. Neither did the Dixons talk much about it to friends.

The ministry aspects of their lives appear as excerpts from letters sprinkled throughout the story. The unselfish and unstinting dedication of Herman and Mary to the physical and spiritual needs of the tribes of East Borneo is indisputable. The statistics speak for themselves. Today there is a church of over 63,000 members in what is now called East Kalimantan.

One can only speculate why the attractive and vivacious Mary wrote this book. Perhaps she had an inner inkling that her life was not long on this earth. Perhaps their shared submission to God and to His will were so basic and indisputed that she simply wanted to reveal a more human, more personal side of missionary life. Perhaps the experiences they shared were indeed too painful, too extreme, too difficult to tell, or the results of their ministry so spectacular it would not be proper to divulge them to casual readers.

Whatever the reasons, readers will find here a highly entertaining and insightful look into the distinct and divergent personalities of two people who loved and respected each other. They also managed to effectively combine their energies and abilities to serve God literally to the uttermost of the uttermost part of the earth.

The following time line brings the reader up to 1948, the point at which this story begins:

1908   Herman Dixon, born May 4, in
        St. Petersburg, Florida

1908	Mary Thornhill, born August 12, in Weston, West Virginia
1929-31	Both attended the Missionary Training Institute (now Nyack College), Nyack, New York Accepted for missionary service Married, September 4, 1931 Pastored The Christian and Missionary Alliance Church in Sharon, Pennsylvania
1932	Sailed for Indonesia from Vancouver, Canada, December 3
1933-34	At Makassar field headquarters (language study, various ministries)
1935	Assigned to Melak, East Borneo (the second largest island in Indonesia; now called Kalimantan), 200 miles upstream from the coast; during six and a half years of ministry there, "hundreds of raw heathen headhunters and demon worshipers turned to Christ."
1938	Furloughed in North America
1939	Left June 22 for Holland where they studied the Dutch language; after four months, they were ordered to evacuate Europe because of the war. They secured passage on the last ship to get through the Suez Canal before it is closed. Left Marseille September 1. Arrived October 23 in Netherlands East Indies (NEI); assigned to Nangah in the Pinoh District of West Borneo, 500 miles upriver from the coast; "baptized scores of believers

and established a number of churches."

1941   Japanese surrounded islands and began to occupy them. "We were so far in the interior that it was impossible to escape."

1942-45   They declined to be hidden by the Dyaks because of the danger it would mean for the villagers; Mary gave her diamond ring to someone for safekeeping; it was apparently retrieved after the war because Mary's sister, Pauline Sexauer, was later given the ring.

Captured in May of 1942 and interned at Kuching, Borneo for 43 months; Mary and Herman were separated in the camp and allowed to see each other only once a month under supervision—only conversation, no touching or any sign of affection;

Mary was selected to divide food for the prisoners. Being very attractive and a missionary, the other women thought she would be fair; she literally counted grains of rice.

Mary apparently was not physically punished but Herman was, sometimes severely. On one occasion he attempted to give Mary a Hershey chocolate bar; he was put in a "dog house" for six weeks, unable even to take care of his personal needs;

The Dixons witnessed horrible atrocities, were put on starvation rations; hundreds died around them; the liberating Australian forces discovered a list of the camp occupants and the dates of their future annihilation.

The following are copies of original postcards sent to The Christian and Missionary Alliance headquarters during the Dixons' internment.

> DEAR ONES:
> SEASON'S GREETINGS! No MAIL RECEIVED. WIFE AND I BOTH WELL. LONG FOR HOME NEWS. APPRECIATE YOUR PRAYERS FOR US AND OUR WORK. LOVE TO ALL.
>
> HOPEFULLY YOURS,
> *Internment Camp, Borneo*
> 25/11/43. HERMAN ALLEN DIXON.

Arrived in the United States August 7, 1944.

> KUCHING, 10/2/43.
> GREETINGS! WE ARE BOTH WELL AND LOOKING FORWARD TO THE TIME WHEN WE CAN RETURN TO OUR WORK AND FAMILIES. YOUR PRAYERS ARE GREATLY APPRECIATED.
>
> HERMAN A. DIXON.
> *Internment Camp, Borneo.*

Arrived in the United States August 7, 1944

> DEAR ONES: Copied from Hand LOC- AND Relatives Letters /B
> GREETINGS. THREE LETTERS RECEIVED—SNEAD, MOTHER, PAULINE—ALL NINETEEN FORTY-THREE. ALSO TWO PARCELS. BOTH WELL. PATIENTLY WAITING. LONGING, PRAYING. BRETHREN, PRAY FOR US. LOVE.
> YOURS IN CHRIST,
> HERMAN ALLEN DIXON
> *Internment Camp, Borneo.*
> CHRISTMAS 1944.

Arrived in the United States Sept 6, 1945

> MAY 19, 1945
>
> GREETINGS. BOTH TOLERABLY WELL. ~~~~~~~~~~~~~~~~~~ HEALTHY APPETITE. LONGING, PRAYING FOR PEACE AND HOME. HOPE YOU ARE WELL. KEEP PRAYING. LOVE TO ALL.
>
> *Internment Camp, Borneo.*
> HERMAN ALLEN DIXON

Arrived in the United States May 19, 1945
Note was censored.

1945   Released September 19 and returned to North America

1948   Returned to Indonesia (the beginning of the narrative of this book)

Information and quotations in this time line were collected from relatives of the Dixons; articles and obituaries in *The Alliance Life*, personal letters written by both Mary and Herman, newspaper reports of their release from internment camp and subsequent ministry in North American churches, and from a small, worn, black sermon notebook belonging to Herman Dixon.

Acknowledgments

In 1954, Herman Dixon, 40 years before his death, bequethed to me the manuscript that has now become this book. His wife Mary, my sister, had completed the story before her untimely death in 1953.

I had been a busy pastor's wife until 1953, when my husband, Earl Sexauer, died. In the ensuing years, life was filled with new challenges and responsibilities.

The manuscript remained in my safekeeping until December 1993, when my niece, Janice Lanpher, her husband Bill and Bill's mother Norma visited me.

In the course of conversation, Norma said, "I think someone should write the story of Mary and Herman's work in Borneo" to which I replied, "I'm holding the manuscript Mary completed before her death." They wanted so much to read it. I consented to loan it to them after being reassured it would be returned.

My appreciation goes to Bill, Janice and Norma Lanpher for getting the ball rolling toward the publication of this book. Thanks a million!

Bill contacted Christian Publications and was put in touch with Marilynne Foster, the editor of *The Jaffray Collection of Missionary Portraits*. She has done a magnificent research and editing job! Heartfelt gratitude, Marilynne.

And thanks to God, our heavenly Father, for His direction in the circuitous route that has resulted in the printing of this story. He is worthy to be praised!

Pauline Thornhill Sexauer
May, 1995

About the Author

Mary Dixon was born Mary Grace Thornhill in Weston, West Virginia, on August 12, 1908. She was the third child in a large family—eight boys and two girls.

While in her teens she became interested in missions through letters written from China by her aunt, Mrs. Georgie B. Minter. Then one day, alone on a hillside reading a copy of *The Alliance Weekly*, God spoke audibly and distinctly to Mary's heart and called her to be a missionary. She was never able to forget that call and in time dedicated her life to Christian service.

In preparation for her life's work, she attended the Boston Bible School, the Beulah Beach Bible School and The Missionary Training Institute at Nyack, New York.

She married Herman Dixon in 1931, and after they had served a church in Sharon, Pennsylvania, they sailed to Borneo in the fall of 1932.

Always refined, Mary was never daunted by sickness, hardships or opposition. She became a capable and zealous missionary for three terms—about 20 years—in one of the hardest pioneer fields. With a Christlike spirit manifested in deeds of love, she won the hearts of Dyak headhunters and was the first white woman to visit many parts of Borneo, the then largely unexplored, third largest island in the world.

During the Dixon's second term they were captured by the Japanese and were interned for 43 months. Separated from her husband, she managed to survive the rigors of internment, although hundreds died in the same camp where she was imprisoned. The Indonesian Mission lost eight missionaries altogether due to the war.

After a two-year stay in America the Dixons were appointed to work in the Apo Kayan District where no missionaries had lived before. Much of this book is dedicated to the telling of their adventures in this desolate, isolated area, where they succeeded in winning hundreds of Dyaks to Christ, then organized them into churches.

While involved in this work, Mrs. Dixon's health broke and she and Herman were compelled to return to America on an emergency furlough. Two years later, on April 2, 1953, she passed away with cancer.

Mrs. Dixon was an eloquent speaker as well as a forceful and interesting writer, and was greatly in demand as a lecturer on missions during each furlough.

Introduction

"Shangri-la" is symbolic of some place along way from anywhere and inaccessible except to only the most intrepid and insistent spirits.

Mary Thornhill Dixon was that kind of spirit. We knew her as a young woman in the Boston Bible School, recently come to the "Hub of the Universe" from the hills of West Virginia; and we knew that she was destined for adventure. She had the imagination, energy, enthusiasm and courage requisite for those who will go far afield in untrodden pathways.

Above all else, she had utter and implicit devotion of heart to the Lord Jesus Christ her Savior who had called her to be a witness for Him somewhere beyond the horizons of her homeland. Willingly, even eagerly, she followed His leading through days of preparation in matters curricular and extra-curricular and, with Herman Dixon, she went to Borneo where both could venture all they had for the Savior.

We followed with deep interest and prayer their pioneer service among the headhunters of interior Borneo, and during the long years of the war, we wondered if they were still alive or if they had been martyred. From that ordeal of living death in a concentration camp for nearly four years, separated as she was from her husband, Mary Dixon came again to America.

The two pioneers could not be content with the narrow frontiers of the homeland but were impelled to turn anew to places still more distant and difficult where heathen hearts still sat in darkness and the shadow of death.

This volume, written so prayerfully and exquisitely, is the record of that new adventure, which ended with an adventure even more wonderful—that abundant entrance into the heavenly kingdom.

There are still places in earth's whitened harvest fields for spirits like Mary's.

V. Raymond Edman
President, Wheaton College
October, 1994

1
Back to Borneo

"Herman, am I crazy or is it the Apo Kayan that's crazy?" Startled at my bluntness, Herman stared at me for what seemed minutes.

"It must be the Apo Kayan," he finally answered.

"Thanks," I responded. "I wanted to be sure. Perhaps both of us *and* the Apo Kayan are crazy."

We had been in the interior of Borneo only a few weeks, but long months before we arrived Herman had tried to prepare me.

"Everything in the Apo Kayan is the most copious, the biggest or the best (sometimes all three) I have ever seen," he had written. "The people are the friendliest, the mountains the most magnificent, the orchids most varied and abundant, the sugar cane the tallest, the rats the largest and fiercest, the dogs the most numerous and savage, the cockroaches the shiniest and rudest, and the leaches, sandflies and mosquitoes the most ubiquitous and tenacious."

One could say that I ventured into the Apo Kayan and its capital, Long Nawang, expecting just about anything to happen to me. And most of it did!

Like a magnificent cathedral, the Apo Kayan (Upper Kayan)—a geographical area exactly as Herman described above—straddles and stretches out and up from the unnavigable rapids which divide the Upper and Lower Kayan to beyond the headwaters of the Kayan River in East Borneo, Indonesia.

Lying between the first and third degrees north of the equator, it is accessible only by native canoes, known as *praus*, or small amphibian airplanes.

Maps—if one is fortunate enough to find maps of interior Borneo—reveal ridges, humps and hills carrying on their business of ripping open rain-bulging clouds to feed the small rivers that swirl over their feet before rushing on to aid the mighty Kayan in its fight to the sea.

Everything in the Apo Kayan is contrary to what one thinks it should be. Nothing acts as it should act, looks like it should look or is what it seems. One naturally assumes that the Kayan River would flow toward the southeast, the nearest route to the Celebes Sea. But not so. It twists and turns sharply north, heading for the China Sea. Then, not liking that direction, it veers northwest before changing its mind again and beginning a long, slow, zigzag curve that ultimately swings northeast. Foaming through rapids and narrow gorges, it finally lies down to flow gently into the Celebes Sea a short distance below Tandjong Selor, the only town of any size along its 400 to 500 miles of curves.

When Herman and I came to the Apo Kayan, we stepped out of our modern world of roads and cars, telephones, stores, clocks, bathrooms, schedules, conventional homes, skyscrapers, newspapers, daily mail, hurrying people wearing beautiful clothes and worry-strained faces, our own race, our families and friends—into a world where progress has been negligible since the arrival of the first inhabitant. And no one could state with authority how many aeons ago the first man came to the Apo Kayan.

We spread out a map. Singapore was to the west and the Philippine Islands to the northeast. Because the map said so, we knew the world was in order. Turning on our radio we could hear voices speaking in familiar English. But as far as we could see and feel, there was nothing in all the universe outside of Borneo's jungle-smothered mountains and valleys.

The painful way to reach the Apo Kayan is by "prau" transport—eight to 12 *praus* in a convoy. Because the lower and upper sections of the Kayan River are separated by an 18-mile stretch of unnavigable rapids, the trip to Long Nawang, the capital of the region and the site of our home-to-be, falls into a journey of three distinct parts.

The *praus* that take off from Tandjong Selor go only to the first of the "bad" rapids on the upriver trip. Here we leave our *praus* for the next downstream group to take back to the coast. Our group makes an 18-mile portage which brings us to the upper edge of the "bad" rapids and back to navigable waters. There one hopes to find a fleet of *praus*. If none are there, trees must be felled and *praus* made before beginning the third part of the journey.

Every trip collects its own assorted experiences. *If* the river does not flood during the trip—but it always does; *if* the paddlers do not have too much dysentery and malaria—but they always do; *if* the portage of supplies does not take longer than planned—but it always does; *if* there are *praus* at the end of the "bad" rapids, so that new ones need not be made—but *praus* are seldom there; *if* no *praus* capsize—but they often do; *if* not one of these misfortunes befalls the passengers, they can expect to arrive at Long Nawang in about two months.

Only three or four of these *prau* transports reach Long Nawang each year. The trip can take up to four months with a loss of from 50 to 80 percent of the cargo. Frequently paddlers die while making the trip and though a man may be fat when he starts, he will be lean before reaching his destination.

The quick way to Long Nawang is by plane.

Ninety minutes after the pontoons of our single-engine Beechcraft tore themselves from the bosom of the Kayan River in front of Tandjong Selor at the coast, Herman and I sat down at Data Dian, the lone spot in the Apo Kayan where the river is sufficiently wide and calm to permit landing. Even here, closely packed mountain peaks make landing impossible unless the plane is small and the pilot is not afraid to die.

Whoever flies this route in a single-engine plane is courting death. The mountains are high, the valleys are deep. Both are jungle-covered. There are no landing strips and the serpentine river is full of rapids and waterfalls. Should the one motor fail, perhaps in time the bodies might be found. Perhaps never!

The climate of the Apo Kayan is cold, hot, rainy, with sudden changes from one to the other. The cold is due to elevation, the heat to the nearness of the equator and the rain to clouds being punctured by mountain spires. I learned never to leave the house without taking either an umbrella or a *saong*, a hat which extends beyond the shoulders and is made of leaves. Within even an hour, I could be sure that either the umbrella or the hat would be used to prevent our brains from being overcooked by the sun or our bodies from feeling as if we are taking an icy shower fully clothed.

Before leaving America we had been told that the Apo Kayan Dyaks were the outstanding people of Borneo. We didn't know any better so we believed what we were told—until we arrived there and learned there are no Dyaks in the Apo Kayan. To call a native of the Apo Kayan a Dyak is to insult him—there are only Kayans and Kenyas.

The Kayans, who are the aborigines, came with the place along with the rivers and jungles. The Kenya tribe embraces 20 distinct divisions, each clinging tenaciously to its name, language and customs.

Both Kayans and Kenyas are the color of heavily creamed coffee, have brown eyes, black hair and stretched ear lobes. My attempt to trace the Kayans and Kenyas back to Adam, or even halfway, was unsuccessful. Since they have no written language, their history has been recorded in their minds, told by the older generation to the younger, to be told in turn to the next generation while sitting around the evening fires. Both tribes are farmers and not many years ago were considered the best head-hunters in Borneo. Just 20 years ago, all were pagan, but now many have become Christians.

During the next three years I would travel up and down the rivers of the Apo Kayan, go to villages where no other white woman had gone, live in homes, share joys and sorrows, sit by fires listening to stories and ask questions until I was thought to be more stupid than their own women—and that made me very stupid indeed, for those women were not considered to be very bright.

2

Goodbye, America!

"Hey, kids, your breakfast is ready!" Dad called up the stairs. What that really meant was that he had made a fresh pot of coffee.

On that morning we had no reason to think we would ever be any nearer the Apo Kayan than we were at that moment. Warren, Ohio, is on the opposite side of the globe. Herman had reached the bacon-eggs-toast stage of breakfast and I the second-cup-of-coffee stage when Dad brought in the mail.

"Besides all the trouble I have getting you out of bed," Dad teased as he held out a handful of letters, "it appears I also have to bring your mail to you."

All the letters were interesting, but the one from Dr. A.C. Snead asking if we would accept an early appointment to the Apo Kayan jerked us abruptly from the roster of post-internment day stars, a role we loved and had played with unique success.

Go back to Borneo? Not us! We had escaped once. We had no intention of being caught out there again. The very thought of it set the still-vivid memories of our internment whizzing on the turntable of my mind. The record then flipped to my last sight of the island.

Our plane had passed over Borneo from west to east. Far below us the island looked like an emerald displayed on sapphire velvet. Borneo's exquisite beauty had always fascinated me, but I saw nothing of her beauty that day. Every flaming oil well, every piece of shattered coastline, every destroyed town and village, every inch of jungle reminded me that down there, underneath that shimmering canopy of green, I had suffered all a person can suffer and live.

Less than a week had gone by since my release. My body was sick, my mind dull. To me, Borneo, humiliation, suffering and fear were so intermingled I could not distinguish one from the other. I had been imprisoned, starved and forced to work like a slave. I had seen people tortured—some into insanity, others into their graves. Malaria, beri-beri, dysentery and tropical ulcers had drained away the last of my health.

When I could no longer bear the sight of Borneo, I determinedly forced my eyes away from the plane's window. But that did not help, for my husband was sitting beside me in worse condition than I. Marks on his body bore testimony that he had been beaten until he was more dead than alive. Malnutrition had affected his eyes until he was temporarily 80 percent blind.

Go back? Of course not!

For days I voiced my resistance to the suggestion. Herman agreed that all my objections were valid, that of course we could not go back. Yes, we could find work to do at home. Of course we could not for the second time expose our families to grief and anxiety because of our being in a danger spot. Besides, we should not be expected to live in the most remote district in Borneo. Yes, war might even keep us from coming home.

I thought Herman shared my hatred for the place, but I was wrong. When I finally cooled down he said calmly, "Honey, possibly there is work for us to do in the Apo Kayan."

"But *we* don't have to do it," I retorted. "You know why we were asked to go, don't you?"

"I'm not sure," he replied hesitantly.

"Well, I am. They were discussing opening up the district and someone, knowing that no doctor lives there and when once in you can't get out, reminded them that the Dixons have no children. Mr. Dixon is good at organizing churches and the natives like him. Let the Dixons do it!"

"Perhaps you're right," Herman admitted, "but don't you think we could give it a try?"

I finally capitulated and we set about to learn all we could about the Apo Kayan.

Books, we soon found out, were always about British Borneo or South Borneo or Java or Bali or Indonesia. Nothing about the Apo Kayan. Half-remembered stories and remarks we had heard in the past emerged to paint a picture of a region so remote and inaccessible that no white people lived there and Indonesian soldiers were not allowed to take their wives with them because of the dangerous rapids on the way.

All American, Dutch and British civilians, seeking refuge at Long Nawang during World War II, were executed there by the Japanese. And, what's more, the Apo Kayan was known best as a sort of red-light district where women came cheap and men took full advantage of the merchandise.

"Necessity," at first a fairly pleasant word, soon became an abomination to me. I remembered how, returning to Borneo from our first furlough, Herman and I had taken all our treasures, heirlooms, wedding gifts and a large collection of books. But, alas, the war had divorced us from all of them.

So we decided this time we would take only "necessities." The list was a long one—everything from thumbtacks to beds. What I considered a "necessity" and what Herman considered a "necessity" were not always the same.

With steel drums, trunks and boxes lined up we began to pack "necessities." My head was so far inside a drum my feet barely touched the floor. Occasionally I could hear faint rumblings.

"What did you say?" I asked loudly and impatiently.

"Are all these sheets, towels and pillowcases 'necessities?'" Herman hollered in response. Or it might be dishes or kitchen utensils or pictures or cushions or clothespins or needles.

"Yes," I would holler back as I dropped once more into the drum.

Once, Herman, eyeing a huge pile of books, suggested we should leave some at home.

"We're taking them," I said. "Of all the 'necessities' we have been talking about, books are the most necessary."

Then looking at his collection of tools and nails I reminded him, "You'll never have time to use all these. Let's leave at least half of them home."

Heaving another keg of nails into a drum, Herman answered, "Can't leave one nail. Everything in that heap comes under 'necessity'."

In an effort to distribute weight, only one keg of nails went into each drum. And for the next four years nails dropped out of toilet tissue, Kleenex and stationery!

Goodbyes are always an agony for me. Frequent reports of war in Indonesia piled fear onto sadness—our own and those who loved us. Friends said we were fools for going back and said goodbye with the finality of someone gazing at a corpse for the last time.

I learned in my teens that all members of all families do not necessarily love each other. But the family I knew was an indestructible one binding Dad, Mother and their eight boys and two girls—William, Clifton, Mary, Raymond, John, Paul, Pauline, James, Harold and Joe—into the compact Thornhill tribe.

We were not perfect but the family ties were. Rarely were we 10 children angelic and certainly never all at the same time. We sometimes quarreled, and we were not above smacking each other occasionally.

Mother did not spare the rod. Dad did, although he, too, used it when forced into action. Clif, short for Clifton, says he is now a preacher and I am married to one because Dad and Mother beat the devil out of us when we were small!

Although William, known as Bill, was the only "good" child of the lot, Clif and I got punished more than some of the others mainly because Clif thought up the mischief and I was his willing accomplice. I never did learn that to follow Clif eventually meant a switch applied to my backside! Possibly the outdoor life we lived on our farm near Hollywood, West Virginia, helped to weld us into a unit. I am not sure of the reason, but I do know that no family could be bound more closely by bonds of love than ours.

Passing years and altered circumstances gave

our indestructible ties flexibility, making possible the adoption of others into the tribe. My aunt, Georgie Minter, came to make her home with us when our mother died leaving 10 children under 18 years of age.

It was late afternoon on January 15, 1948, when Thelma, Paul's wife, came to take us to the train station. Our ship was not to sail until January 21, but we were already a day late for an appointment in New York City. Nothing could postpone this moment of parting—as definite as a period at the end of a sentence.

During the final week, while the telephone rang continuously, flowers and telegrams arrived in profusion and friends visited, leaving with us gifts and their certainty of never seeing us again, my composure, reserved for public viewing, did not slip.

The car was loaded. Turning to Dad, I stepped inside his arms to say goodbye, both of us aching with the knowledge that this might be goodbye forever. Dad opposed our going. He had grieved for us every day and night of our long internment, then had met us in California to welcome us home as children from the dead.

The last words I heard were his.

"Children, you know how I feel about your going, but since you are going, I want you to go with my wishing you Godspeed."

Stumbling out of his encircling arms, with my

composure in shreds and with tears blinding me, Herman guided me down the steps and to the waiting car. Members of the family and more friends than we knew we had in Warren came to see us off. Dad wasn't on the train platform and neither were my brothers. No Thornhill man sheds tears in public.

The next morning we were in New York City. That evening we spent some time at Nyack where once a young Herman Dixon glimpsing the back of a girl's head as she walked into a classroom, promised himself, *I'm going to marry that girl if I can.* He kept his promise.

In stories, in jokes and in men's talk, it is the wife who indulges in shopping orgies. The husband, slaving himself into an early grave to earn the money, is never, never permitted to spend one cent of it himself. How he manages to have even pocket money is left hanging.

But, like a hound chasing a rabbit, his wife is pictured with eyes ablaze, hands wringing and head thrust so far ahead of her feet it is a wonder she doesn't fall flat on her bargain-smelling nose.

With total disregard for the future emptiness of her husband's pockets and his filled grave after he has worked himself to death, she tears through store after store flinging away his money recklessly as she perpetually satisfies her every feminine whim.

This is a false picture. During the five days

we were in New York, I, the wife, avoided shopping—virtually, that is. But Herman, the husband, shopped on the theory that it was his duty to help the impoverished merchants by buying as much merchandise from as many of them as possible!

Herman being to blame for the little shopping I did during those days, I disclaim all responsibility. But, whenever my husband invited me to join him on some of his prowl-for-loot tours, I could not walk the streets with my eyes shut. So naturally I saw the mannequin who, having stood all night long in a store window waiting for me, crooked her finger as I passed by. "Look, Mrs. Dixon," she beckoned, "this dress was made especially for you."

At that very moment, I realized that I really did need another dressy dress. Furthermore, I was dutybound to buy the dress—it would cheer up Herman so much in the jungles of Borneo! Since it is a law of the Medes and Persians that a new dress demands its own accessories, I was literally forced into more buying.

I could not avoid the next step either. Already I had a purse, a camera, an umbrella, a coat, a box and flowers to carry to the ship—and, as no one would expect me to take my new purchases done up in wrapping paper—I was compelled to buy a suitcase. The ones I had brought from Warren were already overfull. Then, because the dress and its accessories did not fill the suitcase, I was pushed into making more purchases which called for visits to several stores. As I went, though, I unselfishly bought Herman a tie here, a pair of socks or a handkerchief there!

"We simply must finish packing today," I announced to Herman the day before our sailing date.

By the following morning, with much packing remaining to be done and our ship scheduled to sail in mid-afternoon, I began to feel nervous.

"Honey, don't you think we should buy some pens for our national workers?" Herman asked.

"No," I replied heartlessly. "Every piece of luggage we have is already bulging like you do after eating a big meal."

"But honey, they will be so disappointed. Say, what do you mean, I bulge?"

"Exactly like your bag there," I replied, pointing to a nearby carry-on which was threatening to burst unless given careful handling.

Later, during a weak moment, I suggested, "Maybe we should buy those pens." Herman slammed the door shut behind him so fast his coat barely missed being de-tailed.

That afternoon the *SS Zeeland* pulled out into the harbor.

Herman and I made up only half of our party. Mary McIlrath and Pauline Roseberry, both going to the islands for the first time, made up the other half. As the four of us stared at the receding shoreline I hugged tightly to my heart the reassurance given me during the last interview my husband and I had with Dr. Snead: Yes, it was safe for a white woman to live in the Apo Kayan. No, I would not be required to wait on the coast while Herman went inland to the Apo Kayan. No, I would not be expected to go through the rapids—a plane would be there to fly me to our home. Yes, the Mission would build us a house and supplies would be flown in. Also, at least one other couple would live in the Apo Kayan with us. Yes, the people in the Apo Kayan were the outstanding Dyaks in Borneo. And yes, at the first hint of trouble the plane would be there to fly us to safety. And on and on.

As it turned out, most of what I clung to at that moment did not come to pass.

3

Hello, Borneo!

It may have been my contemplation of the future that kept me from being seasick for all of two hours—a record for me. I make no claims to being an outstanding person, but when it comes to seasickness, I come first. Or rather, everything comes up first, which causes me to go down first and stay down longer than any other passenger.

I cannot recall how many Atlantic Ocean days went by before I could keep my eyes open long enough to see that our cabin was almost perfect, needing only the clothesline full of fluttering underwear, gaudy socks and nylons we hung diagonally across the room, to bring it to perfection.

As though worn out by giving her impersonation of an attacking tiger and an earthquake all at the same time, the Atlantic finally released us to the azurean calmness of the Mediterranean. Only then did I rise from my bed feeling fairly certain that Herman's time to be made a widower had not yet come.

The *Zeeland*, plowing through the sea like a huge leviathan, was a place of comfort and laziness. This was life. No seasickness. No decisions to make. No pressing duties. A steady ship. Breakfast at 9 a.m. A sun-flooded deck. A lazy chair and a good book.

We assumed the Mediterranean would contribute to our life of leisure by remaining calm. We were wrong—and were surprised when her blue stillness was whipped into abandoned fury.

The ship is rolling; you better go to bed, my stomach whispered to me one morning as I stood up from the breakfast table. I went, but staying in bed was like staying on a bucking bronco. During the few short intervals when I was not fully occupied with being actively sick, I watched suitcases, trunks, boxes and furniture dash to the center of the room and hesitate there an instant before making a crash landing against whichever wall happened to be the underdog at that moment. The clothes, hanging on the line across the room, fluttered and waved, then one by one, dropped from their exalted positions.

Gradually the spasms let go of the ship and unfamiliar noises gave way to normal ones as the storm faded. Looking like a mustard-green slug, I, along with the other passengers who felt and looked the same as I, crawled out to the deck to tell what had happened in our cabin and to listen to news from other sections of the ship.

From that day on, the weather was the kind one reads about on travel folders. No clouds appeared and, with the barren beauty of the Arabian Desert on our left and the equally sandy African coast on our right, we skimmed through the serene dignity of the Suez Canal and the tropics on our journey to Singapore, Java and Makassar.

In Makassar we said goodbye to Polly and Mary at our Mission headquarters. Herman and I planned to stay barely long enough to transfer to a smaller boat which would take us to Tarakan, our last stop before Borneo. However, we now rediscovered that in the East, plans don't often work out according to plan. We had missed the once-a-month boat to Tarakan by one day!

It had been seven years since we had left Borneo because of the war. I felt as though I were looking at the body of an old friend after a terrible accident—torn-away limbs and ripped-open torso. World War II had been over for more than three years, yet Makassar still lay sprawled out, exposing her ghastly wounds.

One day while we were in Makassar, a nicely-worded and neatly hand-written document came from West Borneo. It was a petition sent to the chairman of our Mission and signed by a long list of people among whom Herman and I had lived and worked previous to the war. It was a request that we be sent back to them. The petition could not be granted, but our hearts were touched to know these national friends remembered us. We, however, were on our way to Borneo and to the Dyaks.

Standing on the deck of the *General Verspyck* as it docked at Tarakan, Herman and I assumed that a string of taxis would break away from the clustered oil derricks and storage tanks of which Tarakan appeared to be made, and come bouncing down the wharf to the ship. But no taxis came to help us. This was no pre-war Tarakan. This was post-war Tarakan. So, loaded down like a couple of donkeys, we trudged along the edge of the dock. John Van Patter and Randall Whetzel had come over from Borneo to meet us. Both of them seemed to know what to do with us and our luggage.

Herman had been told that there would be a boat leaving for Tandjong Selor, our jumping-off point to the Apo Kayan, at noon on Saturday. But, true to the usual extendable schedule, the boat did not leave until 8:30 Sunday morning. John, Randall, Herman and I found our spot on a hard bench as the boat rammed her nose into the waves and headed for Borneo.

Tandjong Selor boasts the head government offices and a small, inadequately-staffed hospital. Beside it stands a second-class post office. Everything and everybody going to and coming from the interior pass through Tandjong Selor. To the inland folks this small town looms as great as Chicago to an American. A voyage from their jungle homes to Tandjong Selor holds all the drama and excitement that the world can furnish.

Mr. Lindhout, the Dutch controller, was on the wharf to greet us and to conduct us to the inn. In response to his invitation, we had tea with him, his charming wife Rose and their small daughter Eloise. Mrs. Lindhout told me later that she expected me to come to her tea party wearing a sort of Mother Hubbard dress with my hair in a tight bun at the nape of my neck. The fact is that I arrived wearing a sleek afternoon frock of the current length, high-heeled pumps and a hairstyle as modern as today. Much later in our acquaintance, she told me that she had been very surprised to meet a lady missionary who was able to hold her own in a conversation about world affairs.

When we opened our luggage at the inn, all the smugness we had felt about safely bringing our outfit from New York to Tarakan vanished. Some of the suitcases had been stored below deck against the open drain from the toilet. The odor of stale urine almost knocked us down when we opened the lockers. Most of the contents were unrecognizable because of mold they had sprouted enroute. Only the steel drums arrived in perfect condition except that the radio was dead, the movie camera was stuck, the books were wet, cans of food were rusty and some of our linens were ruined.

"There isn't another place in the world where so many disappointments could be hurled at a person all at one time," I informed Herman one day while in the midst of searching through drums for radio tubes, sunning and ironing clothes, drying tin cans, fretting over the camera and trying to keep down the population we were feeding in back of our house.

Sitting on the edge of a bed with the movie camera on his knees and a screwdriver in his hand, Herman grinned. "I do believe you're right, Honey. We're back in Borneo!"

4

"Necessities" Versus the Kayan River

No sooner had we arrived in Borneo than hints of another separation made us extremely uneasy. The promised plane that would be our lifeline to "the world" had not come, and no one could tell us how many months would go by before it would. So the Mission executive committee appointed Randall Whetzel and Herman to make the initial trip up the river. They were not to wait for the plane.

I was given the choice of staying at Tandjong Selor alone with nothing to do or of teaching in the East Borneo Bible School at Long Bia where I would live with the Van Patters and Mrs. Whetzel.

"Why can't I go to the Apo Kayan with you?" I asked Herman time and time again.

Each time I asked, either Randall or Herman, sometimes both explained that while it might be possible for a lady to make the trip, it would certainly be unladylike. The difficulties encountered would be more than a lady should be called on to endure.

I knew they were right. In all likelihood I would prove more of a hindrance than a help. But to stay at Tandjong Selor during the months Herman would be in the interior was unthinkable. Neither could I face a prolonged wait at Long Bia. Truthfully, I did not want to stay anywhere without Herman.

I was glad, therefore, when the men decided that we should go to Long Bia, 70 miles up the Kayan River from Tandjong Selor, and there I could make a final decision while Randall and Herman made preparations for the trip to the Apo Kayan.

One day John Van Patter said, "Mrs. Dixon, if you will pack the bare necessities, I think we can take them to Long Bia in the outboard-motor *prau*." When Herman arrived I smiled and said, "Our 'necessities' are now 'bare necessities'!"

My husband's eyebrows shot up to where he wishes his hair began as he said, "What do you mean?"

"I mean that you and I are going to do all our packing over again for the 50-11th time—'bare necessities' in one lot for Long Bia, camp equipment and food ready for the Apo Kayan in another and everything else in another to be stored here. Wonderful prospect, isn't it?"

Long before this round of packing was finished, I wondered again why one must invariably do everything the hard way in the East. All our earthly goods had been stored in two small rooms—one upstairs and one down. The heavy pieces of freight had been placed below, cheek to cheek with John Van Patter's drums of gasoline and lubricating oil. The lighter ones were upstairs. But some of the "necessities" were upstairs and some downstairs. And it had to be divided into three lots!

Herman and I dug to the bottom of every drum, crate and trunk we owned. Dividing the contents for its appropriate destination, we then carried it to the location which had been designated for each third.

The Tuesday that a *prau* propelled by an outboard motor and heavy with our "bare necessities" chugged upstream, a sense of great relief came upon me. John and Randall, anxious to reach their families, went with the *prau* but promised to return later in the week for us.

I waited until the first curve in the Kayan River inserted itself between them and us, then proclaimed to Herman and anyone else who cared to listen: "Now we indulge in a few days of rest and quietness."

Sliding into some semi-comfortable chairs we commented how much we were looking forward to the morning we would head up the Kayan River. By evening of that day, of course, we would be at Long Bia and 70 miles nearer the Apo Kayan. Blissful ignorance!

It was four days later when John arrived back at Tandjong Selor not only to take us to Long Bia but to tell us that on the upstream trip the *prau* loaded with our "bare necessities" had sunk to the bottom of the river. One of our foldaway beds, our mattress, pillows, linens, books, office supplies, food and clothing—those "bare necessities" we had so carefully selected and about which I had heard so much—had all sunk into the muddy riverbed.

Despite the fact that the *prau* was too small, the horsepower deficient and the load excessive, we pushed off from shore. All day long, John Van Patter stood in the rear of the *prau* beside the motor, his little daughter Marilyn squatting nearby.

Crouching in the bow, Herman kept a sharp lookout for driftage that might entangle the propeller. Kurung, our lumpish, newlyhired servant, draped himself across the cargo. I sat in the center of the *prau*, a grass mat underneath me, an oil-paper umbrella over me only partially deflecting the white-hot sun from my head and shoulders.

My legs would have been protected had I left my slacks the way slacks are supposed to be worn. But along toward mid-morning I thought, *Now is the time to get a good sun tan.* With pant legs rolled above my knees and sandals off, I inched my bare feet up the side of the heaped-up luggage.

Becoming engrossed in a *Reader's Digest*, I

forgot about my exposed legs until a cramped spine brought me back to reality. The skin on my beet-red legs cracked as I pulled them into the shade of the umbrella and my back assured me it was permanently molded into the shape of a question mark. Herman was no better and perhaps even worse off. His face and arms were already breaking out in blisters.

At noon we ate sandwiches and drank coffee from a thermos without stopping the motor. Then, before we knew it, a cold wind roared between the clouds overhead and the jungles along the riverbanks. And before the *praus* could be covered with canvas, one of the black clouds emptied itself straight down on us.

But that was only the beginning. While it continued to pour, periodically the motor coughed and died, and we drifted at the mercy of the current.

"We can't make Long Bia tonight," John announced as the day waned and the clouds slumped lower.

"Is there a village nearby?" Herman shouted back to John.

"Yes," he replied, "Tendjau is just ahead."

Regardless of anticipating a night without the benefit of cots, bedding and food, I felt any change would be for the better. Nothing could be worse than the wind-driven rain relentlessly hammering us. Or could it?

At Tendjau, the chief gave us our choice of accommodations—either we could sleep in a room with him and his wife or we could spend the night on the veranda of his longhouse. We chose the veranda.

Two Dyak women with brushbrooms stirred up the dust on the floor then carpeted it with a large mat. Cockroaches scampered in every direction as the mat was unfurled. Our suite was ready for occupancy!

Rummaging in our belongings, I came up with a tin of cookies and a can of grapefruit juice. We all shared. Then John and Marilyn lay down on the spot where they had been sitting. That was that. They were "in bed." Kurung pulled his *sarong* over his head and became a cocoon on the floor.

But Herman and I, followed by a crowd of Dyaks, strolled up and down the veranda comparing width and smoothness of floor boards until we found two wide ones side by side. A length of rain-soaked canvas and Herman's clammy raincoat became our mattress. A small, olive-drab mosquito net and my transparent plastic raincoat were our sheet and quilt.

I sat on my side of the "bed" smiling at the Dyaks squatting around us and wishing they would go home. "Dear," I finally said to Herman, "if you tell these people we are going to bed perhaps they will take the hint and go away."

"Why?" he asked. "They like to look at the white woman."

"They can come back when I'm asleep, but first

I want to see if my clothes have become another layer of skin or if they can be peeled off."

"Go ahead," Herman replied. "The Dyaks think nothing of undressing in front of each other. See, they are paying no attention to me," he added, stripping off his trousers.

"It's all right for you to demonstrate," I said. "Your shorts hide what you don't want seen."

"OK, Honey."

Turning to the spectators, Herman said, "Good night, everybody. See you in the morning." But not a man or woman or child moved. Big, brown, unblinking eyes that melted into dots of shimmering velvet in the lantern's light continued to stare at us.

Having learned from past experience that Dyaks can out-sit and out-wait Americans every time, I gave up. Lying down in my wet clothes, I smiled once more at everyone, said goodnight and closed my eyes. Sometime later, when a vomiting dog jarred my eyes open, the Dyaks were gone.

The sun was barely rising along the Kayan River as we chugged breakfastless away from Tendjau. The rain had stopped, the sky was clear and our clothes were still damp on our bodies.

At noon John pointed far ahead to a row of unpainted buildings strung around a thread of green jungle. "There's Long Bia," he announced joyfully.

A burst of gunfire echoed about our ears.

"Are they shooting up the place?" I wondered aloud.

John explained that the lookout man was merely informing the village that we were in sight. They would hastily take their places on the sandbar as the welcoming party.

While still near midstream, John cut the motor, allowing the *prau* to glide leisurely in the direction of the sandbar at the junction of the Kayan and Bia Rivers. I felt we were part of a colossal painting. The canvas was jungle-green, the foreground soft, sandy yellows.

Roofs of houses blended into the distant shadows, and the two rivers rippled along one side and in front. Approaching nearer, we could make out the principal parts of the picture: Warm browns and tans were Dyaks of various types and some Chinese. The lighter tones were Mrs. Van Patter holding baby Janice and Mrs. Whetzel with baby Judy bouncing up and down in her arms. The one splotch of red was Randall Whetzel's sunburned face. A large placard welcomed us.

As our *prau* sidled into the border of the painting we stood to our feet and waved. Instantly the picture sprang into vivid life. The browns and tans splintered into flashing white smiles, the band broke into lilting music and the Americans stepped down to the river's edge to grasp our hands and all talk at once. The change was so rapid we sometimes found ourselves speaking American to Dyaks and vice versa.

We walked to the Van Patter house with the entire village trailing along, the band still playing. My heart glowed. The Long Bia people had received us into their friendship and love.

We were shown to our small two-room apartment. As I stood in the doorway between the living room and the bedroom, I was speechless. Weeks of planning and work and love had gone into making the apartment as nice as possible for us. Add to that the fact that we were strangers to every person in Long Bia except the Whetzels. I was overwhelmed.

The apartment looked like home. Placed tastefully around the room were our belongings that had sunk to the bottom of the river on the first trip.

We will always be grateful to the local Dyaks who without hesitation, we learned, had dived into the cold water, not once but again and again, until the last article had been rescued and lay in a water-logged heap on the bank.

When they arrived at Long Bia with water gurgling from every trunk, crate and box packed in the *prau*, Mrs. Van Patter and Mrs. Whetzel unpacked everything. They washed all that was washable and morning after morning put out to sun things that did not want to dry, bringing them all in each night only to be put out once again the next morning.

Now, eight days after "the sinking," Herman and I found our things neatly arranged in the two tiny rooms made ready for us. But each one of our possessions flaunted scars they would carry to the end of their days. Though stamped "rustproof," all the metal articles were rusted. Colors had run and the linens, draperies, cushions and clothing all showed a uniform mixture of blotched pigments in an over-pattern of mud stains. And no amount of polish would ever make our white shoes white again.

Books, stationery and toilet tissue had reverted to pulp. Files were in pieces. Mirrors looked like they had smallpox. Pictures were blurred. We ripped open the mattress and wrung water from the padding.

Had we been in America we would have discarded the whole *prau* load, but being in the jungles of Borneo, we had no choice but to use everything that remained in one piece albeit discolored and rusty. For three years I hated every one of them!

The village of Long Bia consisted of a few Chinese and a handful of Malays with gardens on the perimeter, plus the buildings and grounds belonging to our East Borneo Preparatory and Bible School. The housing shortage was acute. After the students were provided living quarters and certain sections set aside for classrooms, only one house remained for American habitation. The four Van Patters occupied one of the two bedrooms of that house, the three Whetzels the other. Obviously, there was no room for Herman and me.

But we were there and the missionaries had done their best. Using pandanus leaves in lieu of planks, the men had erected a partition across the *godown* (shed), dividing it into two equal parts. They then subdivided the half reserved for our use into two rooms, moved in the heavy furniture and nailed some shelves to the outside wall.

Where the men left off, the ladies began. They knew how to turn the room with the outside entrance into an attractive living room and the other one into a bedroom. After thousands of cobwebs had been pulled from the rafters and the floor scrubbed with soap and disinfectant, Mrs. Van Patter and Mrs. Whetzel had hung white curtains at the windows, spread lovely quilts on the beds, pinned pictures to the leaf-walls and placed bright rugs on the floor. By the time we arrived, our apartment was ready and waiting. We simply walked in and were home. True, we were not in the Apo Kayan, but we were 70 miles nearer than we had been the day before.

A bell tolled faintly, then Mrs. Van Patter announced, "Lunch is ready whenever you are." As we took our places around a beautifully set table, I thought, *Good for Mrs. Van Patter! She lives in Borneo, but her table could have been plucked from the pages of* Ladies Home Journal.

Looking at the world over a full stomach makes things appear rosy. Thus it was that I viewed our new home, furnished with our ruined "necessities." Until the effect of the meal wore off, I could accept the spoiling of our goods and disregard the nibbling fear that I would not know a moment of comfort so long as I lived in those two rooms.

Time would tell.

5

The Decision

Arriving at last at Long Bia I decided it was time to renew my "accompany-Herman-and-Randall-to-the-Apo-Kayan" campaign. I was hopeful of victory until John Van Patter joined the opposition. John was the head of the school. He needed a teacher and he was convinced I should be that teacher.

Randall finally left the decision up to my husband, glad no doubt that he need not be responsible for another man's wife, especially one with a one-track mind.

When we were alone, I demanded of Herman, "Tell me one good reason why I can't go."

"Honey," he said, "you know as well as I do that the chairman has forbidden you to go."

"Yes, I know, but he is in Makassar," I responded resolutely.

"Mr. Snead also told you not to go until the plane comes," my husband reminded me.

"I know that, too, but he is in New York and

once we are in the jungle he can't order me back."

"Surely you wouldn't disobey our foreign secretary and the chairman of the field!" Herman replied, somewhat aghast at my outburst of rebellion.

"No, not exactly," I conceded, "but the Japanese are the only people who ever kept me from traveling wherever I wished in Borneo and they aren't here."

"I want you to go," Herman said after a brief silence. "You know I always want you with me. But I'm afraid you will collapse before the end of the trip." I knew he spoke the truth. I did not reply. We sat together in the sun-flooded room in silence.

While Herman mulled over the matter in his mind, my thoughts reverted to past experiences in jungle travel which had taught me the full curriculum of discomforts and hardships a lady faces on such a trip.

"Sorry, Dear. What did you say?" I asked, realizing Herman had spoken.

"I said," and he grinned, "if you were any other woman I'd say no."

"But I'm not any other woman."

Herman has the knack of hearing only what he wants to hear and I don't think he wanted to hear my last statement.

"But you have always been able to take it," he continued. "I hope you will be all right. Anyway, get ready and if there is room in the *praus*, you may go." I hugged him and felt sorry for all the millions of women not having a husband like mine.

Our luggage was ready. Every item had been checked off our various lists. Apparently we had everything four people—Randall, Herman, Kurung and I—would need for living 120 days in the jungle far removed from every source of supply. We had packed extra food, kerosene and medicine. Herman and I had learned the hard way that a flooded river means no travel and that low water grounds one just as effectively. Besides, an accident to a *prau*, which is not uncommon when battling rapids, or the illness of even one person can hold up the party for days.

The Kayan River above Long Bia was full of rapids, guaranteed to wash over the contents of every *prau*, to smash *praus* to splinters and/or to drown people. We could do nothing to insure ourselves against any or all of these possibilities except to pack our supplies—including a gift for each village chief and his wife along the way—in waterproof containers.

Randall had ordered the *praus* sent down. As preparations for the trip drew to completion we became anxious to be on our way. Randall and Kurung were awaiting their initiation into jungle travel and Herman and I were about to resume our jungle career after a lengthy absence.

The news filtered up from the river—three *praus* had arrived. *Room for me!* I thought optimistically.

As a rule a large native *prau* is manned by a crew of eight or 10 men. But a far greater number of men filed up the river bank. When asked why so many men had come, the spokesman replied, "Tuan, no missionary has visited us for many years. When we received your letter our happiness was great. So we said, 'It is good for many to go to Long Bia to help bring the tuans upriver'!" It had not entered their minds that they were taking up space the white men might need for the return trip.

One look at the *praus* still loaded with the Dyaks' possessions and I suspected there would be no room for me.

There wasn't.

Much of my work in Borneo had been in the classroom, and I enjoyed it. I was apprehensive, though, of my teaching ability when I joined the faculty at Long Bia composed of Mr. and Mrs. Van Patter, Mrs. Whetzel, plus Miss Bessie and Miss Patty (from other Indonesian islands) and Guru Lilit (a Dyak doing part-time teaching). Very few books in Indonesian were on the market and none of my books or notes had survived the war. I had forgotten much of the technique used in teaching Dyaks and I had hardly spoken the Indonesian language for six years.

My assignment was to teach Bible subjects but I soon found myself including history, geography and current events to the delight and amazement of my pupils.

Young men and women from almost every section of East Borneo sat in the classes, diverse races and language groups, but all children of the jungle unaccustomed to our ways and to education. They had no concept of the present-day world or any world outside their own. The introduction of anything foreign to their simple jungle life called for detailed depiction and dramatization.

Many of the pupils exhibited rare qualities of character and determination.

Guru Lilit was a man with one goal—to complete his schooling which had been interrupted by World War II. Being too poor to pay for a *prau*, Lilit, his wife and three children began the long hike across the Apo Napo Mountain. On top of the mountain, outside the circle of home and friends, their youngest child died. There was no one to weep with them—no one to help Lilit fell a tree, hollow out a length of it for a coffin and dig a grave for the body of his only son.

Guru Lilit and his family arrived at Long Bia in total destitution. Yet, when I met them, they were living in a house they had built. They grew sufficient rice and vegetables for themselves, and Lilit provided meat by hunting deer and wild pigs. With their own hands Lilit and his wife had made a good life for their increasing family.

THE DECISION

In addition to teaching, I had other responsibilities at Long Bia. The only first aid course I had taken taught me how to do little more than to hold the patient's hand and call a doctor. Nevertheless, I took charge of the dispensary.

There was no building to house the dispensary so I partitioned off a section of my living room just inside the front door. Three packing cases labeled Post, Van Patter and Dixon served as storage cabinets and washstands. A wooden bench outside the door became a footrest for ulcerated feet.

An inventory of supplies revealed a scant assortment of drugs and bandages, a thermometer, a pair of scissors with both points broken, a roll of waxed paper, a roll of toilet tissue and a tin of hard candy.

I lacked nearly every item a well-stocked dispensary should have—except patients. Daily I prayed for wisdom and assiduously studied up on tropical diseases. As far as I know, I killed no one. The patients must have spread the word for, according to my diary, I had 421 patients the first month and was up to 675 three months later.

One morning about 5 a.m., I was awakened by "Nyonya Dixon" shouted in a shrill voice at my bedroom window. One leap and I was out of bed.

"What is wrong?" I questioned the shadowy shape outside.

A string of words were shot at me with the velocity of a machine gun. I finally recognized Miss Bessie as the machine gun and caught enough words to understand that Bulan, the Dyak-Chinese adopted daughter of a Chinese woman living nearby, was screaming in pain.

Bulan and I were friends. Many an evening she had slipped into my room for a chat. And often I had felt sorry for her, a 12-year-old child forced into being a beast of burden for her foster family simply because she was half Dyak and adopted.

Noiselessly Miss Bessie and I entered the room, semi-lit by a miniature lamp and the first streaks of daylight.

"Over here," Miss Bessie whispered, directing me to one corner of the room. Bulan was lying on a blood-drenched wooden bench, her lovely face twisted with pain, her eyes wild and afraid. I picked up one of Bulan's hands and placed my other hand on her burning brow.

"Bulan, where are you hurt?" I asked gently.

"Nyonya, I feel shame," Bulan said, making a feeble motion toward her feet.

The foster mother, whom I always think of as "Black Trousers," said, "Three days ago Bulan fell from a tree on a stick of wood which pierced her body. She was picking coffee beans and fell from . . ."

"Where did the stick pierce Bulan's body?" I interrupted.

Miss Bessie pointed to between Bulan's legs.

Despite Bulan's weak effort to keep her blood-soaked, dirt-stiffened pants in place, Miss Bessie and I pushed them down to her knees. The sight was staggering. The lower part of Bulan's body was swollen, discolored and hard. From the torn center protruded a large lump of flesh and clotted, blood-streaked pus. Fresh blood, flowing from around this hideous lump, spread over the bench and dripped onto the floor.

"Why was I not called sooner?" I demanded. "Why did you wait until Bulan was dying?"

"Don't know," mumbled Black Trousers. "We thought she would be all right."

"Haven't you any sense?" I blazed. "Get ready to take Bulan to the hospital at Tandjong Selor. Right now!"

John Van Patter prepared his boat and motor but Black Trousers refused to go along—she couldn't leave her hogs and chickens. I came closer to committing mayhem that morning than at any other time in my life. Only my long-cultivated self-control kept me from shaking that woman's teeth out of her head and giving her a swift kick in the seat of her black pants.

Bulan was in the hospital for a long time, but she lived.

Not all of my patients belonged to the human race. "Since Nyonya Dixon is wise in the use of medicine and she cares for our bodies, she ought to be good enough to doctor our animals." So reasoned some of the Dyaks.

One of my non-human patients was Mrs. Van Patter's goat.

"Nyonya, come quickly. Mrs. Van Patter's little goat has a bad wound," a student called one day.

"How did it get wounded?" I asked.

"Bulan's mother slashed it across its hips with her *parang* when she found the goat in her garden," came the reply.

Black Trousers again! I knew the wound would be serious, for a *parang* is a head-hunting knife and generally razor-sharp.

The kid was cowered against his mother in the students' kitchen. After shutting the mother outside, one of the students forced the patient to be quiet while I cleansed the wound and applied the ointment—all of which started the goat on its way to becoming another of my successful patients.

There were miracles of other sorts at Long Bia as well. Although three families, consisting of four adults and three children, lived in one house, ate at one table, used one bathroom and were always stumbling over each other, I do not recall the slightest disagreement among us. Only God could perform that miracle.

The one wrinkle in my otherwise smooth existence was our apartment. The local folks had done their best to make it bright and comfortable. But the pandanus partition separating our apartment from the other half of the *godown* (shack) utterly failed to provide privacy. With little exertion, a Dyak could easily make a fine peephole simply by sticking a finger through the leaf wall.

In addition, the absence of a ceiling and the fact that the partitions were merely six feet high turned every word we uttered into public property. Another problem was that our rooms, located back of the kitchen where open fires burned incessantly, formed a natural flue for escaping smoke. The smoke took special care to see that our once snow-white curtains and mosquito net were soon turned the color of well-cured ham, not to mention the affect on our lungs and eyes.

The roof owned one virtue—it funneled the water into the rooms instead of just generally flooding them. But with every change of wind the funnels shifted from where I had placed basins to where I had not. When it was not raining, the torrid afternoon sun turned the apartment into an oven.

The WC—short for water closet and European for toilet—was one of those little affairs out in the back yard. I always opened the door with caution, for I never knew what sort of an occupant might already be inside.

One morning a scorpion winked at me from the seat of the commode. With pleasure I flushed him down the drain. Later the same day I discovered a snail in the same place. I sent him down to join the scorpion. Not infrequently the toilet tissue was torn to shreds by monkeys that scaled the wall and crawled in through the opening under the roof.

Neither was it uncommon for the enthroned person to be suddenly intruded upon by the angry chatter of a monkey brazenly glaring at him from atop the wall. The most startling experience was finding the body of a snake festooned across the inside of the latrine. I stayed long enough to locate the head protruding from one side of the building and the tail wiggling outside the opposite wall.

Infrequently canoes came downstream bringing letters from Herman and Randall. They had reached their destination without mishap although flooded rivers had made traveling slow and dangerous. Climbing the Apo Napo Mountain had all but killed the entire party. Thirty-eight days after leaving Long Bia they were given a royal welcome at Long Nawang. And yes, they expected to be back at Long Bia at the end of four months.

A letter to America detailed the trip:

> The trip by *prau* from the coast to Long Nawang usually takes from one to three months, sometimes longer—depending on the condition of the water. But Brother Whetzel and I arrived in 38 days, having actually traveled only 20 days!
>
> Two and one-half weeks were spent enroute, visiting nine of our churches . . . having a two-day convention with the national workers and deacons and baptizing 437. It was good to be able to com-

> fort and encourage our 4,000 Christians in that region who had not been visited by a missionary since before the war.
>
> Since our arrival in the Apo Kayan on June 4, we have not allowed any grass to grow under our feet but have made a circuit of the whole district, visiting 21 of the 22 villages and the nearly 17,000 widely scattered population.
>
> Sad to say there has not been the landslide of converts which we had been led to expect. There was a large turning to the Lord during the war, but not enough national evangelists to teach them and no missionaries to baptize them. Satan took advantage of this condition and since the war a new religion has been introduced called *Burgan Malan*, which is a reformation of the old heathen Dyak religion.
>
> Whole villages, even scores of professing Christians, have embraced this new order ... but Christ and His gospel will triumph in the end. We had the privilege of baptizing 454 (in addition to those on the upriver trip). Also, three Dyak chiefs and one prominent witch doctor believed.

When the four months were almost up I found myself constantly listening for the wild whoop that would tell us someone had sighted the canoe bringing our men home.

Late one afternoon, while I sat at my desk typing, the long-awaited whoop pulled me right off my chair and sent me, accompanied by the entire population of Long Bia, flying to the river's edge.

No canoes were in sight.

"Where are they?" we demanded of the boy

who had run with the message from the next village 15 minutes upstream.

"Oh, they stopped at our village to clean up and change their shirts. They will be here soon," he responded.

He was right. Within a few minutes a *prau* swung into sight loaded with men and odd-looking luggage. All the men looked alike, but as they glided nearer, Mrs. Whetzel and I decided that the two standing in the center of the *prau* must be our husbands. They were a shade lighter in color than their companions, they were the only two not using paddles and, flanked by their loincloth-clad mates—they appeared extremely overdressed in their long trousers and shirts. Herman was home! My world was all right again.

We talked for days. Herman did most of the talking while I put forth great effort to try to understand what he was talking about. I rejoiced with him about the baptisms and turning to Christ that followed their ministry in the villages. Christians in more than half the villages, he said, had been conducting their ser-vices without a single Bible, New Testament or hymnbook. I also learned that of the more than 1600 inhabitants of Long Nawang there were now only 313 believers. The new heathen religion had had its effect there, too.

I knew that the word "long" means "the mouth of any river." So "Long So-and-So" meant the village under discussion was located

THE DECISION

at the mouth of a river by that name. I did not want my husband to suspect that the string of unpronounceable names of villages and chiefs meant nothing to me, nor would they until I actually visited those villages and talked with those chiefs by their fires.

When we talked about our future home, however, I understood perfectly—there was no house in the Apo Kayan for us to live in until we built one.

"Where are we building and what sort of a house?" I wanted to know.

"Randall and I chose a beautiful site," Herman assured me, "subject to your approval, of course. And I ordered lumber to be cut so we can begin to build immediately upon our arrival."

This seemed like a big undertaking to me. Our house was still trees in the Apo Kayan jungles. Hardware and window glass were still in stores at Makassar, Tarakan, Tandjong Selor or America. And the carpenters were still living in some undetermined city in Indonesia.

"Until this house becomes a reality, where do we live?" I asked. "In trees with the other monkeys?"

By turning on his ear-to-ear-smile, my husband softened his slight rebuke. "Honey, you think of the most awful things."

Then he proceeded to tell me that there was a pocket-sized rest house at Long Nawang which the government official said we could occupy while our house was being built. It was dirty, falling down, shot full of holes from the war, ant-eaten and so diminuitive we would not dare fling our arms for fear of knocking out a wall or two.

I was not so sure we could live there. But the alternative was for me to remain at Long Bia while Herman went alone to Long Nawang to supervise the building of the house. We chose life together in the rest house.

Eight months had gone by since we sailed out of New York to take up residence in the Apo Kayan, and still the most complicated part of the venture was ahead of us. Although the Mission plane was due to arrive at Tandjong Selor any day, we surmised that a single-engine plane would prove too small to carry anything of any size. We also knew that there was a good chance that anything sent upstream by *prau* might go to the bottom of the Kayan River or be ruined by long soaking or by being dropped on rocks along the river's edge. Inevitably we knew that one day a *prau* transport would take off for the Apo Kayan loaded with our "necessities."

In an effort to get everything ready for shipment we went to Tandjong Selor. We had been there several days, packing and sweating, when the plane arrived. A distant hum, a small yellow bird circling the town, a perfect landing on the river and our long-overdue plane was there, along with Al Lewis and Bill Conley.

We had last seen Al Lewis the day we sailed from America. And Bill Conley had shared a dressing room with us at Makassar. They were our friends. They had come to Borneo. We were there to welcome them. Nothing more was required to make that day a special one.

A month later everything had fallen into place. The plane was there. Herman had found two carpenters who were willing to go to the Apo Kayan to build our house. A telegram from Mr. Soselisa, the government agent at Long Nawang, arrived informing us that the lumber was ready to begin the house.

Al and Herman began shuttling the "For Plane" pile into Data Dian, the last jumping-off spot before the Apo Kayan. Each time the plane was loaded and took off I tried to estimate how many more trips it would be before I could become an integral part of the load headed for permanent residence in the Apo Kayan. And after each flight I would question the men as to flying conditions that particular day. Their reports varied: good flight, bumpy, poor visibility, rain and ice, stiff tail winds, strong head winds, air pockets, downdrafts or updrafts.

No matter what the current report might be, Al Lewis invariably added, "Mary, I'm going to choose a perfect day to fly you in."

I could hardly wait.

6

The Apo Kayan at Last

Greetings from the Apo Kayan, where both the Dixons have finally arrived!

Yes, we reached Long Nawang on Sunday, January 23, just one year and two days from the time we sailed from New York. It seemed to the very last there was opposition to our coming. The first time we took off from Tandjong Selor we were compelled to return after traveling blindly (instrument flying) for nearly two hours. However, the following day we made it to Data Dian, only to be held up there one day by high water. How good it is to be here in the tiny, crowded two-room [rest house] until we are able to build a mission bungalow.

Recently we had the privilege of witnessing, and Herman participating in, two wonderful ceremonies— the ordination of the first two Dyak ministers in the history of the work. Truly we praise God for these fine men, and we feel this is the beginning of the indigenous church in East Borneo.

The day was perfect. Like diamonds in the sun, the white buildings of Tandjong Selor sparkled under a canopy of sapphire sky tied to earth by distant jungle. The Kayan River ran through the center of the town and in front of the Lewis' house where the plane rode at anchor.

Mary Lewis and I prepared a lunch of baked bean sandwiches and a thermos of coffee. Randall Whetzel—who was going along to help with the plane on the return trip—Al Lewis, Herman and I were dressed in our flying togs and I had with me a notebook in which to record the happenings of the day. This seemed like the perfect day for a flight to the Apo Kayan. Al had kept his promise. It *was* a perfect day.

As I kissed Mary goodbye I wondered if the Apo Kayan would be my Waterloo or if I might sometime have another opportunity to visit Mary in her gracious home.

I gingerly walked across the plank that joined the ramp to the shore, then across the ramp itself and over the back of the seat to take my place with Al in the cockpit. After pushing the plane away from the ramp, Herman and Randall climbed from the pontoons into the back seat as we taxied to the bend in the river for the take-off.

At the upper end of town we roared downstream, kicking high the spray of waves created by our journey upstream. Finally airborne, we circled Tandjong Selor and headed straight for the Apo Kayan.

The whole universe was incredibly beautiful. A silvery filigree of wispy clouds sparkled in the blue dome overhead. Farther inland the clouds looked like snowdrifts snagged on the protruding mountain peaks.

As we ploughed through the drifts without a glimpse of blue or green or any other color, I felt like a tiny doll sitting in a toy airplane, the whole wrapped in cotton, ready for shipment. Surely the words "Fragile," "This Side Up," "Handle With Care" were on the outside.

Visibility had not yet improved when Al informed us that we were now over Data Dian—the end of our journey. We might have been a million miles away for all we could see. So we were not surprised when he added, "Guess we will have to return to Tandjong Selor and try again tomorrow morning." The perfect day had not been so perfect after all.

The following morning we once again soared above town and headed for the Apo Kayan. Near the coast the flying was good, but high over the mountains the same cottony clouds—or some like them—were awaiting our arrival.

We plunged in, flying by instruments. An hour and a half later, the usual time for a flight to Data Dian, there was still no rift in the clouds. Would we have to turn the nose of the plane back toward the coast for the second time?

At the last moment, as we were about to decide to turn back, the clouds rolled back, opening a royal blue pathway straight down to the small space of river where we were to land.

The river in front of Data Dian is narrow and surrounded by lofty mountains. It seemed to me that we fell down an elevator shaft right into the rugged, remote grandeur of the Apo Kayan. According to Al, I snapped open my compact, powdered my nose and combed my hair as though I were arriving in some metropolis instead of the heart of the Borneo jungle.

Doubtless his story is true, but I do not remember much about those moments, for no sooner had we touched the river than my stomach tossed its contents into the bag I carried labeled "For Airsickness."

And so it was that one full year after leaving America we stepped out of our little yellow plane onto the dazzling white sandbar in front of Data Dian amid grinding cameras and a smiling crowd of people. The cameras were there because Mr. Lindhout and Dr. Knapp, an army doctor from Tarakan, had spent some time in the district and were now returning to the coast in the plane that brought us.

Among the crowd were a number of curious people who had come from distant villages to see the new white woman. Here, too, we met Mr. Soselisa, the district officer. From the first moment, a friendship sprang up between our families.

Two other men of note, both native Apo Kayans, were on the scene that day—Baya Jalung, who later became superintendent of all the

Christian and Missionary Alliance churches in the district, and Menteri Whang. The term *menteri* describes someone who is more than a male nurse but less than a doctor. There were two *menteris* in the Apo Kayan—one who stayed at Long Nawang and one who took care of the outlying villages.

The dense, matted jungle pressed in on us from all sides, restricting our world to the river that gurgled around the bottoms of the dugouts impatiently chomping at their bits to be off with us to Long Nawang.

The plane soon became a yellow dot ascending the azure pathway. As I watched it go, something akin to terror gripped me. Our last link with the outside world was disappearing in the sky. Strangeness was on all sides and there was still a three-day journey into the unknown before we would reach the village we were to call home.

With the plane out of sight I concentrated on the people around Herman and me. Joy, sorrow, suffering—the same worldwide expressions—plain human life stamped on every face. They eyed us quizzically. I thought, *Basically, the woman standing here beside me dressed in her fig-leaf-size skirt made of tree bark is the same woman as I am dressed in my blue slacks and plaid shirt. And that man wearing only a loincloth is the same man as Herman who wears trousers and shirt of khaki.*

Some things cannot be explained, which accounts for my inability to explain why I fell in love with those people while we stood together there on that sandbar. But I did and I am still in love with them.

Mr. Soselisa, the district government officer, invited us to make the trip to Long Nawang in his *praus*. We would start early the next morning. At least that is what we planned, but the Kayan River had other plans for us.

By the following morning we had learned our lesson well—no one travels in the Apo Kayan unless the river gives permission. While we slept, the water crept up and up. Daylight unveiled a raging torrent covering the sandbar on which we had stood the previous day and reaching far up the high bank.

"We cannot travel in water like that," the head paddler informed us.

We were comfortable enough in the pastor's house—at least as comfortable as one can be in a house made of handcut boards tied to a crooked framework with rattan strips. During the day we visited with the villagers in their homes and they returned our calls. Different ones presented us with chickens, bananas, sugar cane and firewood. We reciprocated by giving them salt and soap. We also made a present of salt and dried fish to the chief of the village and gave Mr. Soselisa the best gift we could locate—a can of white potatoes.

The river was still high when we embarked the second morning. The current in midstream was too strong to make any headway, but by hugging the shore the men were able to grasp limbs of trees and bushes and pull the *praus* along.

By law every Apo Kayan village is required to maintain a *kubu* for transients. A *kubu* is neither hotel, motel, rest house, inn nor house. If a few planks of incompatible length and thickness, a number of shingles of irregular size and shape and a quantity of deformed tree trunks were piled helter-skelter into a *prau*, then if the *prau*, in shooting a rapid, would ram a boulder with sufficient force to catapult the whole to the top of a high bank where it settled down without architectural finesse—that would be a *kubu*.

The *kubu* at Long Kalang, where we stopped for the first night, was one of the best in the district. It boasted a floor in some places where a floor should have been, a three-foot wall sprouting from the floor in places, a roof hanging overhead in spots and a firebox filled with earth and equipped with stones to serve as trivets for cooking utensils.

While Kurung cooked our rice and heated a can of beef hash for our supper, I helped Herman, Mr. Soselisa and a number of other men arrange our cots. Herman's and mine were placed in the back corner of the *kubu* side by side. Mr. Soselisa's was at the head of my cot so that he and I spent the night with the tops of our heads about an inch apart.

After supper, Herman and the radio entertained the men for a while, but I was too tired and ill to exhibit much interest in my roommates. I didn't mind sharing my room with 21 men or having luminous eyes watching me as I undressed and crawled into bed. That night, at least, my cot felt like the best mattress in America, and my mosquito net offered me the privacy of a locked but not soundproof room.

As though synchronized, the lantern flickered out and the rats came from their hideouts. They danced over the floor and wove in and out of the rafters and turned the hollow post by my left ear into a reverberating staircase. The 19 men occupying mats on the floor neither lay still nor refrained from smoking or talking. They must have felt cold, for not long after midnight they built a roaring fire.

Dogs came in from the village and rattled lids on rice pots and scared the chickens that were tied to the supports of the *kubu* until they squawked loudly. After all of us were fully awake, someone flung a stick of firewood at the dogs and they slinked off, yelping. While 22 unhappy people expressed their sentiments about dogs in general and those in particular, the chickens ended their chorus and only the rats were left to disturb the peace. The whole cycle was repeated several times during the night.

I had not anticipated being riversick. It had never happened to me before even though my fear of water reached almost aquaphobic proportions. But then I had never traveled on such a river as the Kayan, where we laboriously worked through one torrential rapid only to enter another more violent than the first.

Apo Kayan men are clever. They do not require a wife to cook their meals or to plan the menu or wash the dishes. There are none. The men, therefore, are well able to take care of themselves. Every noon our paddlers beached the *praus* on a sand or gravel bar and cooked their dinner. While some of them took care of the canoes, others sprinted into the jungle looking for firewood to make the fire, ferns to cook as vegetables and wide leaves to use for a tablecloth. Poles were driven into the earth to hold the pots and soon the dinner was in pro-cess.

The rice and ferns were quickly cooked, turned out onto the leaves now spread on the ground, and the men took their places in a circle around the mound of food, eating with their fingers. When no more food remained, each man got up leaving the tablecloth on the ground, walked to the river and drank using his hands as a cup.

Skillfully maneuvering the *praus* around a curve in the river early one afternoon of the third day of our voyage, the men set every echo in the mountains chattering with a prolonged yell that almost made me dive overboard. They were simply radioing ahead that we were coming and, at the same time, directing our attention to the village ahead.

"Long Nawang," Mr. Soselisa announced.

Taking my hand in his, Herman whispered, "Honey, we're home."

7

Home with the People

While trying to make the midget government rest house livable—without furniture—for days on end we opened, examined, killed cockroaches, sunned and repacked all goods which had been sent up by prau transport. Alas! Most things had been wet, many articles damaged—a few beyond repair—but we were thankful that the majority could still be used.

Myriads of Christians called on us daily from the town and surrounding villages. We also made many visits and had frequent conferences with the workers. While I shared the regular church ser-vices with Mr. Mangolo (the head district deacon), Mary helped to reorganize the Sunday school at Long Nawang with seven classes. In preparation for this, she translated and arranged a Sunday school program for the whole year, copies of which were sent to each of our workers.

Long Nawang, a village of 1,600 inhabitants, sprawls along the left bank of the Kayan River, facing upstream. An unpaved road herds the houses away from the edge of the river.

At the extreme lower end of the village are the schoolhouse and dormitory. Then come the small homes of the government employees and their families. Next, the public buildings, dispensary, government offices and the minute rest house. Longhouses, bulging with humanity, finish out the village proper.

The army barracks located across the river are not reckoned as a part of the village. They were occupied by Lieutenant Gaillard, a Hollander, and his 40 soldiers of mixed Indonesian races. On the same side of the river live the soldiers' women, only a few of them wives by virtue of a wedding ceremony.

The word "longhouse" defines accurately the overall picture of a native dwelling in interior Borneo. Every house is long, the length determined by the number of people it must accommodate. From the outside, a longhouse, squatting high off the ground on its stilts and with walls and roof out of plumb, looks like a walking centipede.

To go inside, one mounts a log of wood notched in uneven steps and leaning insecurely against the outer edge of the veranda which runs the full length of the longhouse and takes up the front half of the building.

An architect would starve to death where we live. The houses of today are the same as those of 100 years ago—veranda across the front, rooms across the back. The only entrance into these rooms is from the veranda. The center room is larger and has a higher roof than the rest, and rightly so—the chief lives there with his family.

Every room is home to a mother and father and their daughters and their families. When a girl marries, her husband moves into his father-in-law's home. A fire is kept going all night in the fireplace that divides off the bedrooms. A mat placed on the floor is the only mattress the natives know.

I love the verandas. Here, with a fire blazing in a tin-lined box at our feet, I sit on the floor with my friends and listen to stories of earlier days. I watch children romp and play. I hear chickens moving in their baskets, which are suspended from the low rafters, and the soft murmur of pigs rooting in the soil beneath the floor. In some longhouses I see human skulls—smoked black and lined up on a rafter over our heads—and pig tusks—polished white to use as hat racks. And on the verandas we conduct church services until the Christians can erect a church building.

It was not a longhouse, however, that I was primarily interested in the day we arrived at Long Nawang. The only house I could see was the rest house which was to be our home. Herman pointed to the rickety, shedlike building as we skimmed along in front of the village to the landing place.

"Honey, there it is," Herman announced. He had told me it was small, but it was smaller than I could imagine a building to be. We walked onto the porch and Mr. Soselisa invited us to sit down. Then, seeing we had no chairs, he sent to his office next door for some.

News of our arrival spread rapidly throughout the village and soon a welcoming party arrived to greet us—Mrs. Soselisa, Lieutenant Gaillard, plus many natives who timidly gave us their hand and told us they were glad we had come to make our home with them.

As I sat there chatting with our guests, I was two persons. On the one hand I was happy to be there; I liked the people and they needed me. I possessed the peace that comes with the completion of any task. My aim had been to reach Long Nawang, and I had done it. I also knew that God wanted me in that very spot.

On the other hand, I was tired and somewhat discouraged. The mountains crowded closer and closer until they threatened to topple on me. I was dirty and hot. The smallness of the house with its dirt-draped walls depressed me. I wondered how we could possibly live in it.

After the guests had gone I went inside to check it out a little further. There were two tiny rooms fronted by a narrow hallway which ended at the entrance to a shrunken porch leading to the kitchen. The kitchen was furnished with one shelf about shoulder high and a firebox teetering on four wobbly legs and full of mud and ashes.

At the kitchen door the porch turned to the

right past a room used for government storage and eventually led to our bathroom. The bathroom contained a steel drum half-full of stagnant water. The toilet turned out be a high, box-like affair with a small opening in the center. Footprints marked where feet had squatted on the top of the box. A trough connected it to a cesspool in back of the house.

Splintered holes in the walls bothered me—they looked suspiciously like war scars. Later, I learned that once during World War II the village had been machine-gunned by our own forces. That accounted for some of the holes, especially those higher than our heads. The marks of bayonet thrusts in the lower portion of the walls had been left by the Japanese. I did not know where to begin. How could I make a home out of such a house?

Trying to keep out of Herman's way so he could not read my feelings, I wandered from room to room through the cobwebs which draped the walls and hung from the ceilings. In the kitchen and bathroom I swallowed hard to fight back the tears which seemed to want to shake my whole body.

Clearly I could do nothing that day. So I took a bath in the stagnant water, put on a wrinkled skirt and blouse and accompanied my husband to the 4 o'clock church service.

Upon our return from the church service, Herman and Kurung put up our cots in the front room and opened the folding table in the back room. It appeared that we would be living in two rooms—a bedroom and a dining room. By morning, though, I began womanlike to have other notions.

So far as privacy was concerned we might as well have camped out in the middle of the road. Every person walking down the road could see directly into our bedroom—and not one person ever missed a chance to do so. *Why not, then,* I reasoned, *turn this oh-so-public room into a combined living room and office and the second room into a bedroom and use the shaft of the hallway as a dining room?* When I suggested the arrangement to Herman, he agreed. "We don't have any furniture to speak of anyway," he said.

The house had to be cleaned. With the wooden shutters thrown open, the bright light of the morning revealed all of its foul state. Smoke from lamps of former guests fanned out black on the whitewashed walls. Brown stains from a leaky roof traced irregular designs on walls and ceiling. Splotches resembling blood mingled with the others. Grease and sweat from countless hands lay on the doors. Dust and grime beaded every inch of the house, inside and out.

"Kurung," I said, "as I sweep down the walls, you gather up the dirt and scrub the floors."

Sweep down the walls! That is what I did, literally. With the first stroke of the broom a whole section of partition crumbled over my head and fell to the floor. A closer inspection revealed that the partitions were nothing more than two layers of calcimine standing upright. Termites had eaten away the interior wooden supports.

"The house is falling," I called to Herman who was busy opening luggage on the back porch.

The outside walls were in somewhat better condition and lent some support to the structure. *Maybe the whole building will collapse,* I thought to myself. Every time Kurung walked across the floor the house trembled. Well, the walls would have to remain dirty—we would have to get on with the rest of the cleaning. This we did by chasing scorpions, cockroaches, ants and lizards out of corners and scrubbing the doors and floors which still remained strong.

Our furniture was still growing in the jungle, so the folks owning chairs shared an assortment with us. A cupboard also arrived and an old-fashioned showcase which made an excellent bookcase. Tables came in from different sources.

Finally, one day several weeks later, I walked through the house. "It is finished, and it is nice," I said almost out loud.

Surprisingly enough every trunk and box leaving Tandjong Selor had landed at Long Nawang weeks before our arrival. That was a miracle in itself. But the elements had penetrated every one of them. Mrs. Soselisa spread our wet clothes out in the village square to dry and Mr. Soselisa marshaled his office force to police the area for fear some small item might disappear. Of course, we had no secrets left—every one of the 1,600 people in Long Nawang and even some from outlying villages came to view the peculiar things sent in by the foreigners. Our belongings became the main topic of conversation for months afterward, each story growing with the telling.

Many of the dishes were broken, pots and pans dented, linens and clothing watermarked and mud-stained, beds rusted and warped. A large jar containing vitamin pills had broken and the sugarcoating had melted, turning the contents of one footlocker into a syrupy mess. In another, tins of dehydrated blueberries had popped their lids, leaving my underwear with blueberry motifs.

The six-foot kerosene refrigerator we had brought from America did not fare well. At the first portage, the paddlers had lifted it from the *prau* and tried unsuccessfully to carry it along the trail. Finding it impossible, they placed the refrigerator beside the trail, built a leaf-shelter over it and left it there. It spent weeks in the jungles before we could arrange to have another *prau* take it back downstream to the Van Patters who needed a refrigerator as much as we did. We wired for a three-foot one to be sent from Sweden. Eighteen months later it was flown into Data Dian.

There was no telephone jingle in the Apo

Kayan but within a week the whole district knew that Tuan and Nyonya were living at Long Nawang. The entire population beat a path to our door. Standing at the bottom of the steps to our porch, they would clear their throats collectively or cough in unison until we heard and came to take our places at the top of the steps. As men, women and children filed by we shook hands, and to each one we said, "*Selamat Bertemu* (Happy Meeting)." Their reply was a deep-mouthed greeting in one of the 11 languages spoken in the district.

Herman and I sat on chairs while both people and gifts spread out before us on the floor. Bananas were slowly and rhythmically laid at our feet; coconuts, cucumbers, onions and sugarcane were heaped on one side; chickens were put into our hands along with eggs both fresh and rotten. And wild pork—lean and fat and of doubtful age—was given us, along with gardenias and orchids. The news had spread that Nyonya liked flowers.

No word other than the greeting was spoken until the last donation lay before us. Then the chief or his deputy stood to his feet and began a long and loud speech. To Herman and me it was merely a heaping of meaningless sounds, yet we felt sure they were bidding us welcome to their majestic Apo Kayan and offering us their friendship and love.

When the speech was finally interpreted and we could fully understand, I could have wept.

Over and over they thanked us for leaving our rich home in America to come to them and live in their poor, dirty, isolated homes. Our response to their speeches may have lacked some of the flowery phrases they used, but our meaning was just as clear—we were happy to be in the Apo Kayan and we wanted every one of them to be our friend.

Borneo etiquette demands that a hostess serve her guests light refreshments. What could I serve? We did not have enough of any one food to serve the crowds. Fully aware that my reputation as a good hostess would be made by what I served the first group of visitors, I nervously pondered the problem even while I was greeting them.

We had a case of soda crackers, broken and mutilated during their long voyage from San Francisco. We also had several glasses of cream cheese given us two years before by my brother Bill. We had packed moth balls in the same steel drum with the cheese. Now the cheese was generously flavored with moth balls. *Since the natives have tasted neither crackers nor cheese,* I thought to myself, *they don't know what they should taste like.* So I decided to try the first group on the "crackers and cheese á la mothballs."

While Herman amused the guests on the porch, I slipped into the kitchen to search out the largest pieces of crackers and spread them with cheese, one portion per person. The first man took the largest piece and so on until the last one in line had no choice. I winked at Herman and sat back to watch.

Smacking their lips, the guests looked knowingly at each other, jabbering and smiling. I asked the interpreter to tell us what they were saying.

"They like Nyonya's food," he said. "They have never tasted anything so delicious and want to thank Nyonya for deeming them worthy of such delicacies." My reputation was off to a good start!

As the people came to call, and later by going into their homes, we gained fuller insight into their mental and moral philosophy and way of life.

One of the first lessons we learned was not to mention the word Dyak in connection with anyone in the Apo Kayan. That was an insult. Eleven different tribal divisions, each one known by its own name and speaking its own language, occupied the district. But when referring to them collectively we learned to divide them into the two principal divisions—Orang Kenya and Orang Kayan, meaning Kenya people and Kayan people.

The tribes adhere to a rigid class system—the royalty, the freemen and the slaves. The royalty consists of members of Chief Lendjau Djok's family who ruled the whole district from his palace in Long Nawang until his death in 1949.

The freemen are all those not of the royal

family yet not slaves—similiar to the North American middle class. The slaves date back to head-hunting days. Before the Dutch government put a stop to the practice, head-hunting apparently was the main occupation of Apo Kayan men, with slave-taking running a close second. It is the children of the former slaves who make up the slave class of today. They are no longer under bondage but are considered the poorest class. For instance, both freemen and slave class help the nobility plant their rice fields first. Then they all pitch in to help the freemen plant their crops, leaving the slave class until last. Genealogy is not taken lightly by the tribes and there are surprisingly few who marry outside their class. So, once a slave always a slave.

Life for all the tribes follows the same plan. They cut down the jungle and make rice fields—men, women and children spending much of their time in the fields. But this does not mean that both men and women work. There is no fair division.

The men fell the large trees in a new rice field and hunt and roam the jungles searching for fruit. The women do all the rest of the work. With few exceptions, men, women and children chew betel nut, have shiny black teeth and stretched ear lobes.

Almost all the Kayans and Kenyas are satisfied to copy the ways and means of their ancestors. "It is *adat*," they say—customary law, right procedure, conduct, custom. The natives use that statement to answer every question beginning with "why."

It is remarkable how well the tribes get along together, considering that a few years ago deadly animosity existed among them. *Adat* in those days was for men to slip into neighboring territory and take a few heads. The next night the men from the invaded area would retaliate and so on.

In a land where no roads and few trails exist, rivers become the highways. But they are more than highways. From what we observed they are truly the washtub and bathtub for the entire population—as well as the toilet, drinking fountain and swimming hole.

The Apo Kayan—this was home!

8

Plain Living

April 28-30: Conducted the first 1949 three-day conference with our five workers. We discussed many problems and strongly urged the teaching of self-support, also the sponsoring of short-term Bible schools. A session was held with Mr. Mangolo and government school teachers for the purpose of standardizing the writing and spelling of the Lepo' Tau dialect (lingua franca understood throughout the Apo Kayan), which is still not reduced to writing. We then arranged for the translation of the Gospels of Matthew, Luke and John, also the revision of the Gospel of Mark. We further urged the translation of gospel songs and other literature.

With all the national workers present, we held our first communion service for the Long Nawang congregation.

Mary began working on the translation of a 10-day curriculum for short-term Bible schools to be sent to all our workers.

We requested and received official permission to conduct Bible classes in all government schools of the Apo Kayan for a period of one hour per week. At Long Nawang we teach two classes per week besides holding three classes in the pupils' boarding house. We are constantly amazed at how quickly the children can memorize the Word of God!

We had to excommunicate four church members at Long Nawang because of adultery.

"Bare necessities!" Once we had arrived at our destination I had expected never to hear those words again. In reality, however, I was wedded to "bare necessities" for another 10 months until we moved into our own house. Everything not in constant use remained inside drums, lockers and boxes piled in all available places, including the bathroom.

The site for our new house was chosen by Randall and Herman. Finally one day, accompanied by Jahja (John), one of our *gurus* (teachers) and the pastor of the local church, we walked through the village and came out on the riverbank opposite the point on which our house was to be erected. From there I could see only clumps of ragged banana trees and tall grass waving back to the hills.

Jahja rowed us across the river. A close-up revealed a point of land bounded on three sides by the Kayan River, rimmed by tropical fruit trees and backed up against hills with a mountain range beyond. Grass taller than our heads covered the land, broken here and there by tiny spirit-houses.

With Jahja leading the way and pushing the matted grass aside to make a pathway, we walked over our estate, clear back to the little garden of stunted papaya trees Herman had planted during his first trip to the district.

Visitors who were waiting on our porch when we returned to the guest house refused to believe I had made my way through the grass until they examined the cuts and scratches on my legs. Then, with much shaking of heads and pitying groans, they said it was a shame Nyonya's legs were so cut and scratched and that someone should have cut the grass for Nyonya.

When we came to the Apo Kayan we anticipated monthly plane service. Before coming in ourselves we had sent all our supplies and only a bit of food. The rest of our food and the two Chinese carpenters were to come on subsequent flights. To leave the food until last seemed a good plan to us. The monthly flights would insure our having enough to eat. We had also believed the story that "there is not a village in the Apo Kayan where one cannot buy plenty of eggs, vegetables and fruit."

We were wrong on all counts. The plane came to Data Dian again shortly after our arrival, but in less than two weeks the following telegram arrived from Al Lewis: "Had forced landing on second trip. Plane unserviceable. Carpenters returned Tarakan. Must go Makassar February 4. Will keep you informed." Our hearts sank. We were in the middle of the jungle with no carpenters, no mail, no supplies and little food.

After the plane was repaired, Al made a number of flights to the Apo Kayan, but there would be a gap of 13 months before we saw him again. The plane, it seemed, needed more repairs.

Kurung spoke the truth when he said he knew nothing about housework or cooking. But he was willing to learn. I tried to be a patient teacher, but almost from the beginning I sensed certain servant deficiencies: he was slow and dirty in his work habits; he resented correction and seemed at times to be entirely unteachable; He was also allergic to cleaning in corners and simply could not remember from one day to the next what I had taught him the previous day.

On the other hand, his honesty, faithfulness and sincere Christian life soared above reproach. When we visited outlying villages, and church services followed by a singsong kept us up until our eyes refused to stay open any longer, Herman and I could go to bed, leaving Kurung as songleader. He would stay as long as anyone wished to sing.

We accepted an invitation to spend our second Sunday in the district at Long Timunyet, a village located one hour's journey by *prau* up the Nawang River. A *prau* would come for Tuan and Nyonya early in the morning, they said.

It was true. Early in the morning we left to go to Long Timunyet. As we came in sight of the village, nestled among trees along the riverbank, a gong echoed through the valley announcing our arrival and calling the people to drop their chores and come to welcome their guests.

In the time it took to beach our *prau* and climb the notched-log ladder leaning against the bank, walk across a small yard and ascend a ladder to the veranda of a longhouse, the people were already there to receive us.

Beginning with the dignitaries, who stood first in line, we shook hands with every man, woman and child of handshaking age, and patted babies on the head, greeting each one with a word and a smile.

As I went along the line I held some hands covered with scaly rashes, others with cuts and wounds, some wet with perspiration, others dry and fever-hot and every one rough and work-worn.

Some of the people understood our words of greeting, but some did not. We did not comprehend the words they uttered, but we all understood the smile-language used on both sides.

While my husband conducted the church service that morning and I listened to him preach, my eyes were riveted on the dried-out jawbones of nine hogs tied to low rafters along the outer edge of the veranda. I smiled to think how they would upset the interior decoration of an American home and how some of our homeland friends would react if invited to hang their hats and coats on a hog jawbone.

Later in the day, as we strolled through another section of the village, we came upon 48 human skulls smirking down at us from a shelf across the front of the chief's veranda. Some appeared to be fairly recent additions.

That night, with the mosquito net tucked securely around our roll-away beds, the window of the room open to the mellow night air and the house steeped in peace and quietness, we said good night and went to sleep.

Sometime later, something scampered across my bare shoulder, jolting me bolt upright. I grabbed the flashlight we kept between our pillows. Its beam revealed a four-footed animal scurrying down behind my pillow. Holding the flashlight in one hand and trying desperately to open the net, I called to Herman. He sat up, dazed and uncomprehending, until his eyes focused on the animal now in full gallop around and around the inside of the net.

After what seemed hours, we finally managed to raise the net. The animal dashed through, hit the floor with a thud and bounded away. It was the largest rat I had ever seen.

The next morning we bathed in the river along with many others. To bathe with grace and propriety while all the men, women and children of a village either join you in the river or stand on the bank and watch, requires practice and a great deal of agility.

I have seen hundreds of natives bathe and I have been in the river/bathtub with more hundreds, yet I have never seen a completely naked body of a man or woman. Quicker than the eye can see, a man simultaneously drops the last of his clothing, covers his private parts with his hand and dives into the river. He comes out the same way.

The woman wades into the river wearing her wraparound skirt, which she unties as she sits down in the water to shampoo her hair, polish her earrings and wash her skirt. With one motion she stands and ties the wet skirt around her hips.

Here, as in nearly all the villages, the church was a section of a veranda fenced off and dedicated to the worship of God. From the beginning we urged the erection of church buildings, but the natives, deep-rooted in their beliefs that the veranda is the proper setting for all ceremonies, were slow to grasp the significance of a separate building for worship.

To the Christians and to many heathen, my husband became an arbitrator of virtually all their troubles. If only they could tell Tuan, he would immediately offer satisfactory solutions, they thought. I agreed with them. If a solution was to be had, Herman would find it.

At one village we ran into a problem that not even Herman could solve—the eternal triangle of one man and two women.

Early one afternoon, afraid of missing something, I sat down in the chair beside my husband while the eight village elders, the pastor who had come along with us and the man involved in the triangle sat on the floor at our feet. The two women had sent word that they were willing to abide by Tuan's decision, but they did not want to appear in this jungle court.

So far as we could learn, the young man sitting with us had some months previously become engaged to one of the women. Had the pair been heathen, the marriage would have been consummated the night following the day of the proposal, with no ceremony between the proposal and consummation. The government requires and recognizes no legal binding of the Kayans and Kenyas in marriage.

But the engaged couple, being church members and having been taught that the right way to begin married life is with a Christian wedding ceremony, decided to live apart until one of our *gurus* could come from another village to marry them. But the district was large and the *guru* was long in coming. While the couple waited, the young man was discovered sleeping with another girl.

"Now, Tuan, how shall we settle this case?" the spokesman for the elders asked.

"What is your tribal law covering such actions?" Herman countered.

"It is up to the guilty man to pay a fine to his fiancée."

"All right, make him pay the usual fine," Herman advised.

"But Tuan," the elder responded, "he has paid the fine and his fiancée is not satisfied. She wants more."

"Here we go," I remarked to my husband out of the corner of my mouth.

It took an interminable time to glean the real facts of the matter from many drawn-out speeches and lengthy cross-examination. I listened to one prolonged, rambling speech after another, gathering only a trickle of information from each. When the last word had been uttered, I asked Herman, "Do you suppose the whole story has been told?"

Neither of us could be sure, but we had gathered these facts: The engaged girl accused the *guru* of being responsible for the downfall of her fiancé. Had she not been a member of the Church she would have become his wife in less than 24 hours after receiving the proposal. Therefore, although she had not lived with the man, she considered herself his wife. Because she looked upon the man as her husband, she felt he ought to pay her the tribal "husband fine" in addition to the "lover fine."

Darkness fell and still Herman had not found a satisfactory solution. He never did.

Several weeks later, after visiting a number of churches, we were safely back home. "We did have a good time," I wrote in my diary, "except for my river sickness and Herman's suffering with malaria."

Now that a delegation from each village had visited in our home and we had been entertained in all the villages upstream, we hoped to be granted a few days of no visitors and no great demands on our time and energy.

However, our hopes were not realized. Before even the bedding used on our trip was laundered, we received a telegram from Al Lewis informing us that the plane had been repaired and requesting Herman to meet him at Data Dian as quickly as possible.

Two days later, Herman, still suffering from a fever, left for Data Dian. He promised to be home on the fifth day—one day downstream, one to visit with Al and three for the return trip.

I stood on the sandbar and waved until the *praus* were out of sight. Then I went straight to bed. For the next five days I spent my time either in bed or in a classroom. We had begun to teach Bible classes in the five grades taught in the local government school. I felt it was my duty to be there and do my part even though I did not feel well.

By the fifth day—the day of Herman's homecoming—I felt better and decided that life might be worth living after all. But Herman did not come that day, nor the next. On the morning of the seventh day I knew my husband could not reach home that day. The river had become a torrent overnight. No *prau* could survive the tempestuous waters that roared past our doorway. And besides, Herman had packed only enough food for a five-day trip. I worried he might be hungry.

The river continued in flood all the eighth and ninth day and didn't begin to recede until the 10th. Herman did not come that day either.

At noon of the 11th day I was sitting at my desk writing when I heard the voice I love most in the world coming from the front veranda.

"Anyone home?" he called playfully.

I wanted to run into his arms, but with a porch full of people watching from next door I waited until we were inside the house.

The *praus* were filled with letters, magazines, newspapers and parcels from home—our first mail in six weeks. As we opened the packages, Herman and I chuckled to ourselves.

Herman had lived on rice and ferns during his lengthy trip upriver. I, too, had been short of food. Our "rice-stomachs" could hardly stand the veritable feast of North American food that greeted our eyes as we opened parcel after parcel.

God was good!

9

A Great Chief Passes

Pe Lendjau Djok, aged king of the Apo Kayan, died. The general alarm was sounded, gongs were beaten continually which caused great excitmeent. Alas! He died not a Christian, although several times he declared his willingness to believe should his village advisers give consent to follow suit. All work in the village was suspended for 10 days while hundreds of men labored to carve an elaborate coffin and erect an imposing mausoleum.

Chief Lendjau Djok, chief of all the Apo Kayan, died in his palace at Long Nawang, June 11, 1949. Death was due to old age and a broken heart.

Known throughout the district as Big Chief, Chief Lendjau Djok had ruled long and well. Under his guidance, war and head-hunting had given way to peace and order. Doing away with head-hunting was not natural to Chief Lendjau. He learned the hard way that Holland did more than frown upon the practice.

In the early years of the century, Holland

founded an army/government post at Long Nawang. Being a young chief, inexperienced in the attitude of foreigners toward right and wrong, Lendjau Djok gave permission to some of his friends to "take heads." He went to prison.

The story, often repeated to us, is this.

A kind, mild man, the chief himself had never "cut a head." He enjoyed living quietly in his palace, going occasionally to his smaller house at the edge of his rice field to see how his crop was progressing. He sometimes expressed fear of the changes brought to the district by the new-fangled government. He was soon to find out how the Dutch viewed head-hunting.

One day, some of his subjects came to him from a village near the border of British Borneo. A group of Iban Dyaks had foolishly crossed the border. They were received politely into a longhouse, given the customary cigarette-of-friendship and told to stay as long as they desired. The welcome seemed so cordial and they were made to feel so comfortable that they overstayed their welcome. Even while their hosts were smiling, runners were on their way to Long Nawang to seek permission to "cut their heads."

"They are there right now," the runners excitedly told the chief. "What shall we do? Cut their heads or not cut their heads?"

Chief Lendjau was in a tight spot. His culture taught that certain ceremonies require human heads. He could see nothing wrong in fulfilling the requirement. He feared demons would inflict sickness and death on his people if fresh heads were not offered in sacrifice from time to time.

But the chief had been warned that cutting heads would result in punishment. Pondering the problem from every angle, he reasoned that since he himself would not be doing the beheading and the village where the deed was to be executed was far away, the government would never know that men had lost their lives. These men living in the barracks and sitting behind desks in the Dutch offices knew neither the language nor the ways of the people, and no one would talk about the heads.

"Take their heads," Chief Djok finally decreed.

The heads were already off and hanging in a cluster above a firebox in the process of being smoked before the government agents even suspected a breaking of the no-head-hunting rule. Investigation traced the guilt back to Chief Lendjau Djok. The next several years of his life were spent in prisons outside of Borneo.

After his release, Chief Djok returned to the district. He was now, in the opinion of his subjects, an even more powerful ruler. He had braved and conquered the dangers encountered in the outside world. In his own mind the chief was convinced head-hunting must cease and that it was his duty to stamp out the practice in his district.

To stop head-hunting was a difficult thing. To Chief Djok's people a human skull contained the strongest supernatural powers in the world. The newer the skull the greater the magic. A skull, skillfully manipulated by the hands of a witch doctor, prevented too much rain from falling or made enough fall as the need might be. It also caused rice fields to flourish, scared wild animals away, kept sickness and death from invading villages, warned away other tribes' evil spirits and endowed the tribe's leaders with knowledge greater than other men's. Signs of a skull's decreasing power called for a fresh head, while the old one took its place above the fireplace in front of the chief's room.

Under Chief Djok's wise leadership, overt head-hunting stopped and feudal tribes learned to live together in unity if not in love.

Christianity came to the chief's district, brought first by nationals who had become Christians while at Tandjong Selor. Later, *gurus* came to live among them and missionaries made infrequent visits. Still later Herman and I arrived to make our home with the chief's people.

We often visited the old man in his palace and he repaid the visits whenever he was able to walk, which was not often. Down through the years changes in the district had sickened his heart. The final change and, I think, the one hurting him most, happened toward the end of his life. The village leaders refused to donate a part of their rice crop to him, thus breaking tribal custom. The old man's heart broke under the insult. His children no longer loved and respected him. He wanted to die. And finally did.

As though death released a spring of compassion, his subjects grieved over his passing. Runners took to the trail to publish the death notice in overland villages and *praus* sped word to settlements along the riverbanks. As each village heard the news, another set of gongs joined the gongs at Long Nawang which began to moan the moment the chief died and continued for 10 days. A weird throbbing and sobbing of gongs permeated the mountains, rivers and jungles of the entire Apo Kayan.

Herman and I were told we might view the body of the chief just as soon as he was properly dressed. Anyi, one of his grandsons, led us to the palace. The veranda served as a funeral parlor and looked like a county fair. The glory of a splendidly built, strong man had departed from the shrunken, wizened man now lying on a cot. His frail body could not fill his old-fashioned Dutch Admiral's uniform and his gold-braided cap was several sizes too large and stood out from his head.

He was surrounded by his treasures—yards and yards of garish cloth and brightly colored rugs with a tiger, the family emblem, prominently displayed on them. Gorgeously ornate head-hunting knives, his clothing and beadwork, his throne, his spears—all were on display near his body.

My husband and I gazed at our friend from the foot of the cot. Then we knelt beside him, along with weeping and lamenting natives. Our grief, although quieter, was as sincere as theirs. Reduced by death, the common denominator to plain human beings, without race, creed or language—we all knelt together around the bier of our Big Chief.

The same day the chief died the body was placed inside a hastily prepared coffin. On the third day the coffin was sealed. The people began to flock in from every village in the district to participate in the death ceremonies and laborious preparations for depositing the body in the death-house specially built to be the final resting place of the ruler of the Apo Kayan.

Witch doctors, aided by assistants, gong music and much sacrificing of pigs and chickens continuously and loudly besought the spirits to grant their beloved chief a safe and peaceful journey to the spirit-world. Strong young men were dispatched to search the jungles for the largest tree in the district and, no matter how far distant the tree, they were ordered to bring it to Long Nawang.

The tree was located far away and downstream. I wondered, watching the men battle their way up through rapids with the tree trunk lashed between two *praus*, how they could exert enough strength for such a herculean task. Designated workmen set to work to turn out the most elaborately carved and gaudily decorated coffin the combined forces of the district could produce. The women beat out rice and cooked food to feed hundreds of guests. I believe the Soselisas and Dixons were the only ones not working on something related to the chief's interment.

Normally Christians bury their own dead and the heathen theirs, but Christians and heathen alike helped prepare the coffins and death-house and lined the pathway from the palace to the death-house while their chief made his last journey.

By afternoon of the 10th day all was in readiness for the final ceremony. The smaller coffin was placed inside the large, highly decorated one, which was then sealed with pitch. The combined weight was almost a ton—weight to be carried for nearly a mile on men's shoulders.

Disregarding straining muscles and groans of the men beneath the burden, several men of the royal family rode atop the coffin. Some of them waved flags, but one took it upon himself to beat any man suspected of shirking his share of the load.

The death-house, a small square building, sat on four huge pillars with a ramp leading up to it from the ground. A section of the roof with

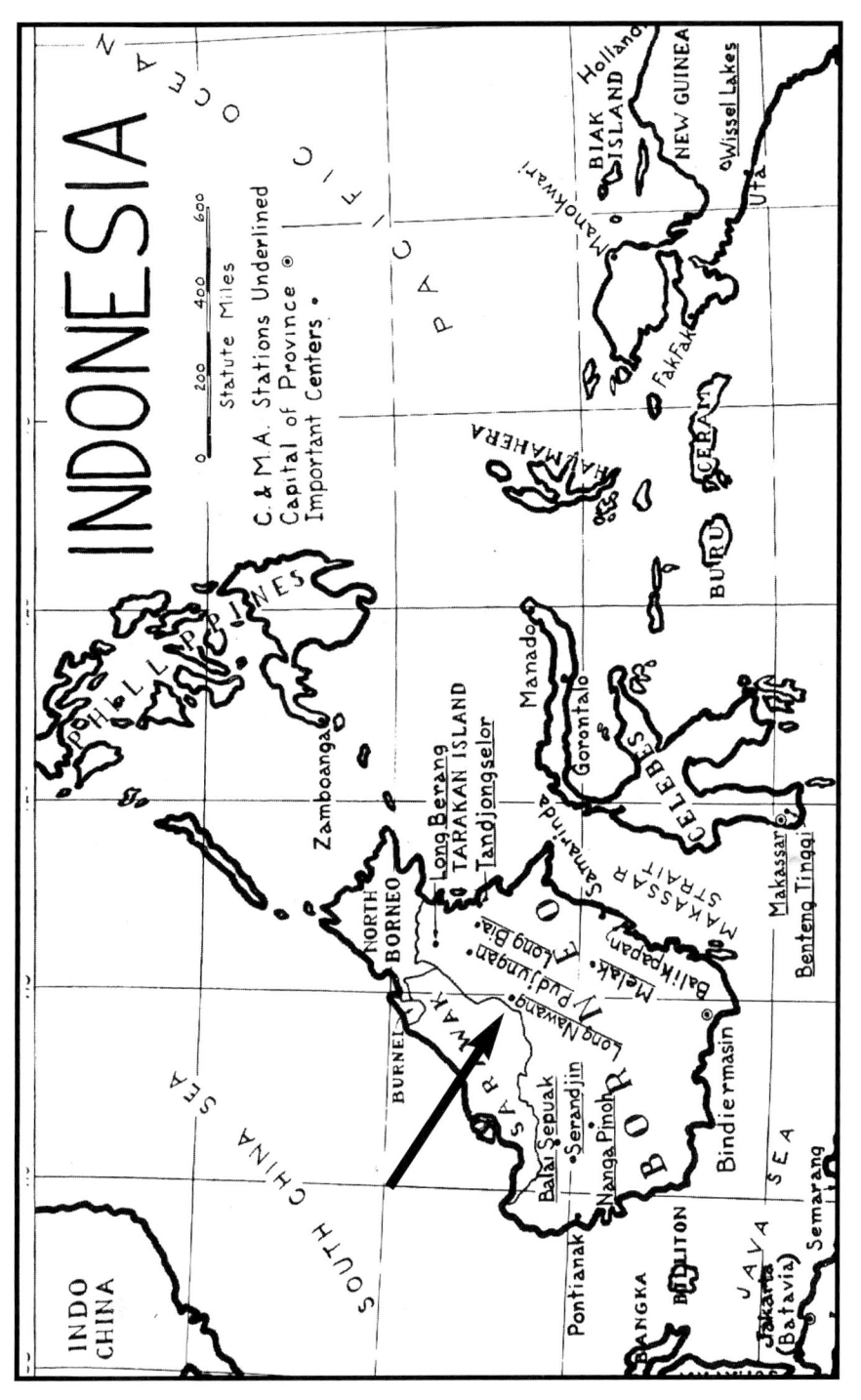

Map of Indonesia. Arrow indicates location of Long Nawang.

Herman and Mary Dixon in 1932, as they left for
Indonesia for their first term.

Herman and Mary Dixon on their way to Borneo, 1947, after two years at home following their internment experience.

The Mission plane taking off from Tandjong Selor.

Government buildings at Long Nawang. The rest house, first home of the Dixons, is on the left.

Kurung, the Dixon's servant.

The *menteris* (male nurses) in front of their clinic at Long Nawang.

A Dyak welcome at Data Dian.

Mary with four Dyak schoolboys and two servants—their Borneo family.

A Bible training class at Long Nawang.

The treacherous Apo Kayan, the only highway to the coast, 500 miles away.

Christian Dyak paddlers say grace at a sandbar.

Shooting the rapids on the way to Long Bia.

The house on Mission Point.

Mass grave at Long Nawang of missionaries martyred by the Japanese.

Dutch Shell Oil flying boat which evacuated
the Dixons for their final journey home.

Herman and Mary in 1952, home for the last time.

its rich carvings of serpents, tigers and birds had to be removed in order to get the coffin inside. Straining every muscle, the men inched their way up the steep ramp and lowered the coffin to the floor of the little house.

Speeches followed and good-byes were said as one by one the chief's subjects left. Finally, only his widow stood in the death-house. She, too, slowly turned and crept down the ramp. Within minutes the room was closed and the roof replaced. Big Chief's throne, knives, shields, trunks, jars, cloth and clothing were arranged on the narrow veranda facing the river. The old chief was left alone high above the Kayan River where everyone traveling the river would look up to the tomb of a mighty chief.

The chief was not a Christian. We had repeatedly urged him to become one but his answer was always the same: "Christianity is fine for my children, but I am too old and tired to change."

Forbidden to "take heads," he continued the outward rites of his heathen religion, but he confessed to feeling it had little meaning. Acquainted with every *bali* (spirit) that rules a person from conception to death, he observed all ceremonies due them while deploring the time and means spent in such observances. Perhaps during the days he lay beside his firebox, drowsing toward death, he thought of the myriad *balis* that had ruled his life. *Balis* are always evil spirits. The people of the Apo Kayan recognize no benevolent god.

The river *bali* causes both high and low water. When the river is in flood or almost empty, that particular *bali* must be given pigs and chickens. These are hung on stilts along the riverbanks.

Disease arrives at villages borne on the wings of a *bali*. The only method to keep the *bali* away is to encircle the village with a band of ceremony in which a generous supply of blood is used.

When rice is planted, while it grows and before it is harvested, the *balis* demand offerings.

Childbirth, sickness and death call for appeasement of the *balis* held responsible for such.

Thunder growls in the skies when the thunder *balis* turn the heavens into a bowling alley. *Balis*, the people believe, roll stones down the skyway and as they roll along some of them crash together and thus produce claps of thunder.

The red eyes of a *bali*, angry with the world, are the rainbow. If anyone is compelled to go outside while the flaming eyes of the rainbow *bali* look down from the sky, a hat large enough to cover head and shoulders must be worn to deflect the fiery darts of the spirits. Should the red eyes fall upon an expectant mother, her baby will die.

Bali Kak, the spirit of childbirth, watches over a child until birth. His work is then done and the child is given a period of freedom, the only freedom from *balis* it will ever know. From the moment of birth until three days or perhaps three months—depending upon whether the family is planting or harvesting rice or have chickens and pigs for a proper feast and ceremony—the baby has no *bali* and no name.

During this time—three days to three months—the mother and child remain inside the house. But when the name-day comes, the child is carried outside. A chicken or pig is slaughtered and the blood is smeared on the arms and hands of the baby. A name is given the child, and a *bali* entering the child on his name-day directs every action of his life. A non-Christian fears nothing more than to displease his personal *bali*.

As the child grows up he learns there are myriad *balis* to be honored and pacified. Should *Bali Uman*, the spirit of food, be slighted, famine and death will follow. A *Bali Uman* abides with each family in a large urn in each room of every longhouse. Natives have declared to us that truly if a family breaks any rule connected with the worhip of *Bali Uman* some member or members of that family will die or become insane.

A ceremony to *Bali Mamat* is a sort of rearmament scheme. In earlier days, the Mamat ritual was observed each time men returned from a successful head-hunting expedition, thanking Mamat for his help in taking heads and asking for a ceremonial cleansing to prepare for future head-hunting trips. No women participate in this ritual but from what has been told me, the women did their share of dancing, drinking, carousing and eating after the men finished.

But with head-hunting ruled out, the Mamat ritual was merely a ceremonial cleansing and a renewal of strength should enemies invade the district or permission be granted to return to the "good old days."

Every year an ordinary trunk of a tree changes into a Mamat totem pole called *belawing*. A deep hole is dug in the top of a prominent hill and a live hog is lowered into the hole. The bottom of the pole is placed on the back of the hog and both are buried deep in the earth. Once in place, the pole is decorated according to local taste, but always a hornbill bird—a symbol of strength—sits atop the pole. When the totem pole is decorated to everyone's liking, they dance and chant and go into all sorts of contortions considered necessary for receiving a renewal of warlike prowess.

Three years have passed since the death of Chief Lendjau Djok. No one has yet been chosen to take his place. But what can one expect? Only three years have gone by. That is scarcely long enough for such a momentous choice to be made in the Apo Kayan.

10

A White Lady Doing Nothing in the Tropics

It seemed to be the general consensus that white women have nothing to do in the tropics and that if a white man wants to live happily there, he either stays a bachelor or he leaves his family elsewhere.

I think there is some ground for such a consensus. Some women do not have sufficient work to occupy their time and minds. I have seen them in the coastal cities trying to fill in the hours of the day by playing bridge, shopping and gossiping—and complaining to their husbands that they were very unhappy. I always felt they would be just as unhappy anywhere else, for happiness comes from the inside and not from without.

However, I am not fit to judge other such white women, for I neither live in a coastal city nor do I have any spare moments. If I have been a handicap to my husband, he has overcome it and his work has been highly successful. I may not have been so successful, but I have labored too, disproving the theory that white women do not work in the tropics.

Nurse. "Mrs. Dixon is willing to do her best in taking care of sick people." This news item preceded us to the Apo Kayan. No sooner, therefore, had we landed than patients began to come to our home and I took on the role of nurse.

The government offices separated our house from the government dispensary where two male nurses, Whang and Lawai, lived. Those two boys had been most unlucky. A few months prior to our coming, they had pushed off from Tandjong Selor with a *prau* load of medical equipment and supplies. En route, their *prau* capsized in a rapid and they lost everything. With all those months gone, there still was no medicine at the dispensary.

For some reason many of the natives seemed to have more confidence in my ability than in that of the *menteris*. In actuality, Whang and Lawai were better trained than I was, and they could talk with the people without using an interpreter. When I found myself entirely out of my depth, I called in the army nurse who knew more about medical science than any of us.

Almost without knowing what was happening, I found myself giving out quinine for malaria, chasing worms from swollen stomachs, giving sulfa for pneumonia, dressing wounds and ulcers and washing out eyes and ears.

Herman and I were standing on our porch one day about noon talking with Mr. Mangolo when Whang landed at the bottom of the steps. He was so frightened and excited he stumbled over his words. We managed to pick up enough to learn that early that morning a baby had been born but the placenta had not delivered. The baby was all right but the mother was dying. Without pausing to change into more suitable shoes I rushed down the steps to join Whang.

We started running. I knew we needed to take a shortcut so I headed up the notched-log ladder of a longhouse and at full speed ran the length of the veranda, my high-heeled shoes clicking on one end of the loose floorboards as my weight raised the boards from their unattached end.

Darting down the ladder at the far end of the veranda, I ran on and up the steps of a little house, across that porch, fought my way through a room full of assorted sizes and genders of people and into the second little room just as full of assorted sizes and genders of people.

By the light filtering through the one small window, I saw the newborn baby, still unwashed, lying on the floor against the wall, wailing. The mother was tied to a board with two men at her head holding the board at such a slant that the poor soul was all but standing straight up.

She was unconscious and had swallowed her tongue. Several men and women were punching her abdomen. Someone was trying to force her to take a drink of water. A pair of men kept calling her name. Her husband stroked her hand. Blood covered the floor.

Pushing the people aside, I ordered them to leave the room and made my way through the blood to the mother. A quick examination confirmed that she was beyond anything I could do for her.

"Someone call the army nurse," I demanded.

He soon arrived and worked over the patient for a long time. Ultimately the woman's tongue was back in place and the placenta delivered. The mother opened her eyes and asked to see her baby.

A year later, while we were out of the district, she died in childbirth.

It seemed to me that half of the people in the district had goiter and every one of them came to us for iodine. Somewhere they had heard that iodine was a sure cure for the disease. One woman brought me two eggs—one was rotten—and begged me for some iodine.

"Yes," I said, "I will give you some but don't take more than I tell you to take each day and mix it with a cup of water before drinking it."

"All right, Nyonya," came the reply.

Repeatedly I showed her how to count the drops and she promised faithfully to carry out my instructions. I thought it was safe to give her a month's supply.

A couple days later she was back with an empty bottle and two more eggs—both rotten.

"What did you do with the iodine I gave you?" I inquired.

"Well, Nyonya," she answered, "I wanted to get well quickly and so all day long I took little sips from the bottle. Now it is all gone."

I wondered how much iodine it would take to kill an Apo Kayan native!

Young women sporting brown-tinted fingernails caused me to be suspicious. I was not surprised to discover that their iodine was being turned into fingernail polish!

And then there was the man who insisted that I give him two large tablespoons of castor oil. I have not seen him since!

Language Learner. My second seemingly full-time career was language study. We had spoken the Indonesian language, which was the accepted vernacular throughout Indonesia, almost from the dawn of our years in the islands—up to this time, a total of 17 years. And, until we went to the Apo Kayan, this one language, with a smattering of tribal dialects, adequately allowed us to meet every demand.

In the Apo Kayan, as elsewhere, the educated class speaks Indonesian. All formal teaching is done in that language. But, with a vast majority of the inhabitants in our new district being unschooled, we were compelled to begin the study of an unwritten language. By sifting through the 11 different tongues spoken, we were able to come up with Lepo' Tau as a sort of *linga franca* understood by most of the people.

Lepo' Tau was unwritten and no two people agreed on the pronunciation. Anyway, just try reproducing the pronunciation of someone who has a mouth full of chewed-up betel nut with juice and words flowing together!

Guru Ilung was our first teacher. He spent his days teaching in the public school and then came to us late in the afternoon. I think he may have been a fine school teacher but when it came to teaching foreigners a new language, he was lost. After we had taught him how to teach us, we all got along better!

After studying Lepo' Tau for a while I appreciated my mother tongue more than ever. I could say what I wanted to say, knowing that when I ended a sentence I had said what I started out to say and that each word in the sentence had a meaning. Not so with Lepo' Tau! Going over our written work, Ilung would insert several additional words.

"Why do you use that?" became our stock question.

"It has no meaning," was his disconcerting answer. "It is a flower-word, put there to make the construction beautiful."

At the end of two months Ilung had to give up teaching us. For the third time he developed active tuberculosis and had to enter the hospital at Tarakan.

Lendjau, a handsome Eurasian government worker, became our second and last teacher. He proved to be such an interesting conversationalist and could relate such a wealth of folklore that we often forgot to make "sentence bouquets full of flowers" and talked in Indonesian just for the fun of talking and learning the origin of the tribes and the history of the district. And eventually we were able to communicate sufficiently well to carry on our work.

Teacher. At Long Bia I had taught at the Bible school. In the Apo Kayan I continued to be a Bible teacher, but now my classes were taught in the public schools, in a girls' school and in church. And, as at Long Bia, teaching the Bible meant teaching a variety of subjects.

The Indonesian government was in the process of being born during our days in the Apo Kayan. Nationals throughout the archipelago were trying out their newly won independence from Holland. And in the Apo Kayan the people were waking to a consciousness of a world outside their mountain home.

An education is costly in the Apo Kayan—not in money, but in hardship. Since 1928 the government had maintained schools in some of the larger villages. Nearly all of these schools offered classes through the third grade. The Long Nawang school had recently advanced to include the sixth grade.

Shedlike dormitories, built near the schoolhouse, sheltered boys coming in from outlying villages to attend school. Girls attended school, too, but they generally lived in the homes of relatives or friends. The government provided some food in the classes but the majority of the children had to supply their own food or walk daily from their home village.

Little boys, too young to even be separated from their mothers, took care of themselves, cooking their tiny pots of rice and squatting beside the river washing their clothes. Many of the boys, apparently no more than eight years of age, were completely on their own. They lived in one room, did their own cooking, washed their clothing, grew their vegetables and made whatever money they had. Many of them were very sweet children.

More than 95 percent of the school children came from Christian homes. The heathen could not see the need of an education—their ancestors were not educated—and they did not agree with this new-fangled idea that a child should waste his hours in a school room when he could be working in the rice field.

Twice a week I taught classes in the girls' school, a subsidiary of the churches in the district. And every Wednesday evening I had a Bible class mixed with down-to-earth advice for the women. We called it "Mothers' Meeting." I also met with the local Sunday school teachers on Saturday afternoons to drill into them the Sunday school lesson they would teach the following day.

With my days full to the point of bursting their seams—keeping house, entertaining visitors, calling in homes, participating in church services, carrying on an extensive correspondence, doing bookkeeping, studying a foreign language, taking care of countless sick people and teaching classes, I felt confident of ineligibility for the title, "A White Lady Doing Nothing in the Tropics."

11

Massacre at Long Nawang

When the Japanese arrived on the shores of Borneo in 1942, a number of people including Americans, British, Eurasians and Hollanders fled from the coastal towns to the safe sanctuary of remote Long Nawang where Holland maintained an army post.

Among the refugees were Mrs. Bumphries and two children from British Borneo, and Mr. and Mrs. McPherson and child, also from British Borneo. Rev. and Mrs. Sande and their baby, and Rev. Fred Jackson, Alliance missionaries, also came. More than 40 men, both army and civilian, completed the roster.

The difficult-to-reach Long Nawang, they felt, would offer the one place in Borneo where life would be safe, a refuge until the war ended and they could be restored to their homes and loved ones. Food might be a problem but there would be enough. The natives could be persuaded to sell rice and vegetable gardens could be planted. No one believed the Japanese would consider the tiny outpost worth military effort.

Nothing occurred for some months to interrupt the serenity. But suddenly, late one afternoon, a Kenya man rushed into the village. The first thing he reported was that soldiers of a different sort from Holland soldiers were coming. The second thing he needed to do before the strange soldiers arrived was to snatch his daughter from her home and the arms of the soldier with whom she lived and take her back to her hidden home in the jungle.

The commanding officer rejected the man's story and told him he was either mistaken or lying about having seen "short and stubby with shaved heads" soldiers. The Kenya did, however, take his daughter away with him and, although the officer rejected the report, some of the soldiers believed it.

They begged permission to ambush the Japanese, declaring they could successfully defend a mountain pass through which the enemy must come. This permission was refused, as was their plea for extra ammunition.

For several days there were no reports of sightings nor any other indication of the arrival of the Japanese. Then, early one morning, the local soldiers climbed to the top of the hill on their side of the river for their routine drill. But there was no drill that morning or ever again for many of them.

No sooner were they in position than a volley of gunfire issuing from the corresponding hilltop across the river killed a number of them and put the rest to flight. The Japanese had come silently during the night, set up their guns and by daybreak were ready to take over the village.

All army personnel and foreigners were taken prisoners. The Indonesian soldiers were subsequently freed but their Eurasian officers—in fact, everyone possessing even a drop of "white" blood—was slaughtered.

Francina Davids lived with the Sandes and recounted the following story as she became an unwilling witness to the horrors in the wake of the Japanese invasion.

"The morning the Japanese came they called all civilian men to the office saying they wished to interrogate them. They were not permitted to go home but were imprisoned in the barracks where the army was already imprisoned. A couple of days later, Mrs. Sande and I were ready to sit down to lunch when two Japanese soldiers came for Mrs. Sande and her baby. That day, Mrs. Sande and Mrs. Bumphries and their three children were placed into another of the army barracks. Mrs. McPherson and baby were left in this rest house. She had been wounded the morning the Japanese came and could not walk.

"A week later, the men—first the soldiers, then the civilians—were led out of their prison to a narrow valley nearby, were forced to dig their long-trench graves beside the pathway and then were shot.

"About a month went by and the Japanese declared a holiday. Every native living at Long Nawang, they said, must go upstream out of sight of the village to witness a demonstration of army tactics. Hand grenades were to be thrown into the river to kill plenty of fish for all to eat. The day would be a picnic.

"The Mangolos and I had been allowed to care for the McPherson baby because the wounded mother was unable to do so. But on the night before the holiday the soldiers took the baby away from us, giving the excuse that the next day the women and children would be sent downstream to an internment camp. The same evening, Mrs. McPherson was taken across the river to join the other women in the barracks.

"When the village people, following their Japanese leaders, headed for the spot some distance upstream, Mrs. Mangolo and I hid ourselves so we could watch our foreign friends leave for the camp. From time to time we heard blasts of guns going off upstream but as we peeped through a crack in the Mangolo house we could see no *praus* in the process of being made ready for a trip.

"We were still watching when the door of the barracks flew open and the women filed out behind a guard. They did not march toward the river, however, but turned into the valley, walking the pathway their husbands had walked a month before.

"Soon Mrs. Mangolo and I could see them no more. With the next burst of gunfire upstream came another from across the river behind the little hill where the women had gone.

"That evening the natives returned to the village and nothing was said about the happenings across the river while they were away. Subsequent investigation proved that the women and children had been herded along the pathway skirting the trench where their husbands and fathers were buried. On a little farther, beyond the path cutting back to the cemetery, they were halted and shot, their bodies falling into the ravine flanking the pathway. Throwing a light covering of earth over the warm bodies, the soldiers returned to the barracks, their day's work done."

The Japanese had exacted the supreme penalty for belonging to the enemy nations and had returned the bodies to mother earth. But as Mrs. Sande said to Francina, "They may kill my husband's body but they cannot touch his soul."

Herman and I had been at Long Nawang only a short time when we crossed the river and walked back to the cemetery where our dead rested. One of the first acts of our returning army had been to take the bodies from the ravine and give them a proper burial in a mass grave in the military cemetery.

As we walked softly along the pathway it was easy to picture the happenings of those days back in 1942. In the churchlike stillness of the green valley it seemed the dead walked with us. Leaving the barracks where the prisoners lived, we were almost immediately between two low hills that form a natural gateway to a lovely, narrow valley. Beyond the gateway the path curves around a hill to the right. Neither the barracks nor the village can be seen. One is alone with hills and sky.

We stood on the spot where the army officers and Fred Jackson—considered army because he was the pilot of our plane—were lined up on the left bank of the path and shot. The slashed earth still showed where they had been buried.

A few steps farther on we stopped beside the spot where the civilian men had been killed. Between the two, but to the right of the pathway, we saw the graves of two Japanese men who had lived at Long Nawang when the war ended and were executed by the natives.

Then we went on, crossing the opening to the path leading off to the left and ending at the cemetery where the women and children had been halted and shot. There we could see the disturbed earth—their place of sleep from 1942 until our returning army took them up and laid the three groups together in one grave. Surely they deserved to share a final resting place, for they had shared in life, in imprisonment and in death.

Turning to our left and passing between two more low hills we came to the military cemetery, a beautiful site like a deep saucer with a dais in the center. Mountains formed a fluted edge around the dais, the cemetery proper. Standing beside the grave and contemplating the loveliness of the surroundings, not a person in sight, not a sound except birds singing in the trees, the warm sun beating down on the scene, I thought, *This is perfect. Restful sleep away from the hustle and bustle of the world. These folks thought they were fleeing to safety, and they have found it here in this circle of pristine perfection.*

Once more, however, they were to be disturbed. Before our first year in the Apo Kayan ended, Lieutenant Gaillard was ordered to ship the bodies of our war dead to Tarakan to be reinterred in the war memorial cemetery. There they rest today.

12

"Paradise" Lost and Gained

In what portion shall we mix the black and the white in order to paint a true picture of the Apo Kayan and events since our February letter? The name of the picture is "Troubles and Triumphs."

We were not here long before we recognized that our former experiences had not adequately prepared us for the Apo Kayan. We have felt like new missionaries with everything to learn. Here the country is mountainous, the people different, the language strange and unwritten; we are more isolated; fresh food is unobtainable most of the time. (We are wondering if we shall become dehydrated from eating so much dried food!)

We are meeting problems never before encountered. These are caused partly by young Christians being ignorant of Bible teaching and partly by no one with authority living in the district to settle problems. Thus, it has been a case of every man doing as he pleased.

Yet these months have been so blessed by God that this period might well be labeled Genesis, the beginning of many things. And we are trusting that the end will be even greater and mightier than the beginning.

October 11. Received one five-gallon oil tin of

[mail]. Alas! the soldered tin had rusted from being in the water so long and was full of tiny pin-holes. Thus, the mail was wet and dirty, but still legible, praise the Lord!

When we tried to put the glass into the window frames of our house, we found much of it broken in transit from the coast. Also, approximately half of the five buckets of house paint were either lost or ruined by water!

December. It does not seem like Christmas according to the scenery and circumstances: so hot and green, no presents and little food. But good services and Christmas program. After all, it is the heart condition which really matters, and we desire to give Him the worship, praise and adoration due Him at this season—and evermore!

The rest house became the dispensary after we moved. Some days while I passed the house and greeted the sick people sitting on the veranda, I relived the time Herman had almost died and the time I was ill while we lived there.

One night I awoke gasping for breath, feeling that huge hands were tightening around my throat, choking me to death. As days and nights went by, my throat became progressively worse and I wondered if the end was near. I was not looking forward to choking to death.

My husband tried to be brave but I know he was afraid, too. I think we had reason to fear. The plane was unfit for a trip to the Apo Kayan and the local wireless had no batteries. We could not send an SOS, nor could help come to us.

When we first came to the Apo Kayan someone had told us: "If you ever are really stuck you can come down by *prau*. It isn't like being completely cut off." Of course, that alternative was utterly ridiculous. The person in need of help would either be well or dead long before the trip downstream came to an end.

So I fought to keep breathing. The walls of the house pressed in upon me until I felt held in a vise. Blood spots on the walls mocked me. The bullet holes and bayonet wounds leered at me. The mountains seemed to push against the house, and there was no sky—only discolored ceiling pressing onto my bed. No one knew of our plight and certainly no one cared.

At the end of two weeks I was finally able to breathe normally. The battle-scarred walls shifted back into place, the ceiling retreated. Life seemed good again.

Returning from the border of death made me more aware of life. Relationships took on a higher value and the senses penetrated to new depths and with new perspective. I felt that everything in the world was right and beautiful.

Herman's brush with death was not too far behind.

"Honey, will you come here?" he called one day a couple of minutes after he had gone to take a bath.

I made my way to the bathroom between

stacked-up trunks, boxes and drums, thinking it strange that my husband had called.

Pushing open the door I opened my mouth to ask, "What is it?" but got no farther than, "What . . . ?" Herman was sitting on the toilet, naked, face pale as death and body red as fire from his toes to his waist. In the midst of telling me that he had suddenly felt sick, his eyes rolled upward, his head sagged and he slumped toward one wall.

Instinctively I reached for his glasses with one hand while throwing my other arm around him. He was already unconscious. I was sure he was dying. I did not know what to do.

There was no one within calling distance. My arm was all that kept him from collapsing in a heap on the floor, so I could not leave to call for help. I prayed. And I watched as his face grew old and pinched.

About 10 minutes later Herman looked at me, at first with cloudy eyes, then more clearly. As soon as he could sit alone I bathed his burning body and helped him to bed. I no longer cared about the unsuitableness of the rest house for human occupation. I did not care that our new house was slow in building. Not having a good assortment of food did not bother me. I did not care that we needed a multitude of supplies for ourselves and for our work. All that was important was that my husband had come back to me.

Late one afternoon a *prau* transport arrived in pouring rain. Much of its load belonged to us. The paddlers, their arms and backs loaded down, filed by our house on their way to the office, their tired and hungry bodies staggering as they walked.

They had left Tandjong Selor 98 days before, expecting a quick trip home. But floods had come. Some of the men had nearly died en route. Even now some of them were ill. Their rice had run out, and they had been hungry as high water held them fixed on the riverbank for days. They feared much of the cargo was ruined by torrential rains that had beaten upon them almost every day of the return trip. A part of the load had been dropped into the river and one *prau* had capsized in the rapids.

The next morning, in brilliant sunshine, I went over to the office to examine the cargo. It was obvious that what had left the coast was much larger than the few pieces I was seeing. However auspicious the start, the end result was a sorry mess.

I couldn't find any medical supplies, so I went to the dispensary to inquire if once again no medicine had been included in the shipment.

"A little," Lawai told me, "but most of it was lost in the rapids. And I do not know what I have—all the labels have been soaked off."

"Let me see what came," I said.

A few jars of vari-colored salve stood on a table flanked by some cartons of pills already minus their sugar coating, swollen and wet. Sick at heart I walked out of the dispensary, not knowing what to say.

Later in the day a roar from Lawai brought me running to find him furiously waving his arms and chasing the largest of the billy goats across the yard.

"What's wrong?" I called to him.

"Nyonya, I put those pills out to dry in the sun and this crazy old goat came along and ate them all!"

Although it was truly a sad state of affairs, I could not control myself. Soon we were both laughing—we hoped the pills were poison and would kill the goat. No such luck! If anything, he was more rambunctious following the pill episode. Maybe the pills were vitamins!

The contents of our *prau* load fared no better than the rest. Our only case of fruit rested on the bottom of the river. One five-gallon tin of kerosene had leaked until it arrived empty. All of the oil tins had also sprung leaks. Half of every can of paint was water with a scum of oil floating on top.

My greatest disappointment was the tomato sauce. For a long time I had anticipated the day we would have some tangy tomato sauce to add a little flavor to our rather tasteless food.

"Leave the other cases," I told Herman, "and open this one so I can use a can of sauce for lunch."

What a letdown! Instead of tomato sauce, there were 72 bottles of hot sauce! Chili peppers grow practically wild in the Apo Kayan. I could have made all the hot sauce we needed.

There were other annoyances, too, in the jungles.

Spiders and I fought a daily battle. Each morning I discovered the furniture laced together and anchored to the floor by filmy but tough cords. Typewriters wore gossamer. Clothes had to be pulled loose from the same webs which also adorned lamps and flowers and curtains and eaves.

The dogs and I, too, were incessantly at loggerheads. It seemed to me there were 50,000 in the district and that every one of them came sometime or another to Long Nawang and to our house. While conceding the fact that the people could not live without dogs for hunting, I failed to appreciate dogs being placed between children and spouses in the lineup of human affections. Anything with food in it had to be hung from rafters to avoid the marauding creatures. And they often lifted their legs on our door jambs even as we tried to carry on a respectable conversation with their masters.

Goats and I did not get along well either. They fought under our house; they sent lumber and shingles flying in all directions; they shook the house by rubbing against it. Worst of all, they bumped their heads against the floor beams beneath our feet. I could have cheerfully murdered them.

Chickens and I closed each day with a truce that broke down the following morning. They flew through our windows and strutted through our doorways into living room, dining room and bedroom. They ate every edible substance from stalks of bananas suspended from rafters to the soap on the shelf.

Ants, sand fleas and mosquitoes and I also carried on a constant blood feud. By day we wore a liberal coating of insect repellent and by night we slept beneath a mosquito net.

Rats and I were deadly enemies. Their ubiquity rivaled that of the chickens. Moonlight seemed to give rats insomnia. Night became their favorite time to play tag all over the house. One evening as I read in the living room a family of rats waltzed through the front door. I decided not to disturb them even though they almost touched my feet as they played their games. Finally they left by the same door they had entered.

Scorpions lurked under every piece of furniture, box and drum and between books. They nested in lumber beneath our house and crawled over the floor.

Yes, the early days in the district were full of joy, sorrow, regrets and disappointments mingled together to become plain living. I can think of nothing that expresses my real response to those days so well as these words I wrote while we resided in the rest house:

> True, the rest house is an unpleasant place to live. But with the last class taught, the last service conducted, the last guest gone, the day is ended and all is still except for an occasional laugh or word floating in from one of the nearby houses.
>
> We shut the front door, light our lovely lamps and pick up the book that we laid down the previous night. Then, sitting in the soft glow of the lamp, we lose ourselves in beauty. The light span does not sufficiently outline the falling-down walls or bring out the blood stains there or illumine the lamp-smoked smudges. It centers my husband and me in a mellow white glow of radiance.
>
> News of strikes and unrest does not penetrate this atmosphere. And wars being fought in many places in the world, as near to us as South Borneo, are too far away for us to realize. Yes, troubles and sorrows harassing the world at large do not touch us.
>
> Here we know a peace and contentment that we failed to find in America, in Europe or in the coastal towns of Indonesia. Here, together, we spend an hour that needs no artificial excitement. For we know the day now closing its pages forever has neither been spent on self nor in self-interest. Others have been helped by our coming to the Apo Kayan, and there are people out there in the darkness who are better because we came.

13

Mission Point

At present an assault is being made on our ears that will probably leave us deaf for the rest of our lives, in addition to driving us crazy, so that in the future our friends will excuse our queer actions by saying, "Poor Herman and Mary! They are a bit tetched from having lived too long in Borneo!"

Well, it won't be caused by our living in Borneo, but rather by being smothered in a feather bed of racket. All around us hammers and nails suffer head-on collisions; saws rip boards asunder; rough planks shrilly resist the plane; glass cringes before the cutter, while emitting a cold-water-poured-into-hot-oil sizzle; words in four languages stab the din, the grumbling of our poison-tongued carpenter weaving the whole into a screeching pattern.

Possibly you have guessed that we are living in the new house. Yes, four days ago we moved. Although the house lacks many finishing touches and our few pieces of furniture look like lily pads floating on a vast ocean, we are enjoying most unusual comfort. The floor is safe to walk on; walls do not shed scraps of their being every time the wind blows; space allows us to hold our arms out full-length without knocking down partitions. Early in 1942 the Japanese broke up our home life. Now, living in this house gives us the feeling that we are home again.

Knowing that in case of an emergency there is no way out of the district in time to do any good has not tended to make us feel comfortable. Before one can start downstream at least a month is required to collect paddlers, canoes and rice, then from two weeks to a month (depending on the river) to go to the coast. Thus, by the time we reached Tandjong Selor the emergency would not exist.

The day we arrived at Long Nawang one of our guests, sitting on our front veranda, jestingly remarked, "Nyonya, you are living on top of your house."

I remembered the thought that had gone through my mind the first day we arrived: *Those piles of lopsided shingles beneath the rest house are about the most unsightly things I have ever seen.* But when I heard that those rough shingles were the roof of our new house, they suddenly became endowed with a special beauty which no other shingles ever possessed. Yes, we were literally living on top of our house.

When Mr. Whetzel and Herman paid their initial visit to the district, our house was still growing in the jungle. Every board and every shingle was still a part of a tree, waiting to be cut down and cut out by hand. Mr. Soselisa promised to have natives go into the jungles, prepare the lumber and bring it to Long Nawang. And, true to his promise, he had the lumber cut—actually hacked—and stored beneath every public building in the village.

One of the happiest events of our lives was the beginning of the building of our house on Mission Point, as we named the site of our new home. We had not lived in our own home since the day, eight years before, when the Japanese had taken us from our home in West Borneo. Now, at last, within a short period we would have a house of our very own.

Herman and I felt like a bride and groom anticipating their first home. It was probably a good thing we could not fathom the difficulties separating the beginning from the completion. The entire eight and a half months required to build the house could have been a period of happiness had Chu A Kie, the head carpenter, not been so ill-tempered (actually, I think he was the vilest-tempered person I ever knew), continually yelling at his hapless helpers until they fled and refused to work again. The workers were an ever-changing crew, untrained and clumsy. In all the months we knew "Acid-Tongue" (alias Chu A Kie), I uncovered only one good trait in him—he did put in a full day's work.

Juk Chiu, Acid-Tongue's younger brother, was a charming rascal. He had been at Long Nawang only a short time when he came to Herman with a "very important request." He had proposed marriage to a local girl and she was willing to become his wife—provided my husband performed the wedding ceremony.

Herman was dumbfounded. He knew that Juk Chiu had a wife and baby at Tarakan. According to Juk Chiu, that was all right: "This marriage here is to be a temporary one." Naturally, Herman refused to perform the ceremony and the girl refused to be his wife.

The lumber for our house, it turned out, had not been hacked down to the required thinness. Every piece called for recutting, which resulted in our paying twice for each piece of timber used in the house. While the workers hacked away on the boards, Acid-Tongue raved at them. They did not work fast enough. The boards were not even. The men were "dumb." They would never learn.

Now, a Kenya or a Kayan is a proud man. He does not have to work. His life is reckoned good if he has enough rice to eat, dogs with which to hunt and children to carry on his name. The only money he needs is to pay taxes; so why work longer than the few days necessary to earn the exact amount?

Nails! How can such a small, humble article be of paramount importance? Herman had bought such a quantity of nails that I thought our house would be made of nails. But before the framework was up, we ran out of nails of the correct size. With the roof partly on—no more shingle nails. With the walls and floors incomplete—no more nails.

Frantically we wired Al Lewis to fly in nails. In the meantime, Herman and I pulled out of the rest house every nail that looked like it might do. We borrowed from the army and the government. We ripped apart boxes and crates for nails. It was not that Herman had failed to buy sufficient nails, but, with some of them going into the house and some into the pockets and loincloths of the workers, we were continually searching for more nails.

Of one thing we were sure—we had plenty of lumber on Mission Point. There would even be some for furniture once the house was finished and we had a place to put it.

Then, one night about midnight, "Cha, Dua, Telus (One, two, three)"—followed by grunts and sounds of *praus* scraping the ground—snapped our slumber in two. The Kayan River was rising fast and the villagers were pulling their *praus* to higher ground. Actually, our neighbors were tying theirs to the posts beneath our bedroom.

Soon much of the village was under water. We did not worry about our new house, however, for it was built on a knoll. The next day we found that the house was all right, but much of the lumber had been swept away. A review of the scene confirmed our suspicion that not only was the lumber for our furniture gone, but we lacked sufficient lumber to complete the house. Back to the forest for more hacking.

Mr. Soselisa had drawn up explicit plans for the house. Acid-Tongue said he could easily follow the plans. But mistakes plagued us all the way. Two doors were cut in the wrong places. The front veranda turned out to be more than three feet narrower than planned. The office was to have been smaller than the two bedrooms, but all three turned out to be the same size.

Repeatedly Herman told Acid-Tongue to use the best lumber in the front part of the house; the knotted and worm-eaten wood would do for the back, if necessary. When the floor was laid, directly in front of the front door, two holes, rotted through and discolored around the edge, stared up at us.

Getting a window in the bathroom and another in the kitchen cost many days of battle. "You don't need a window in either," grumbled Acid-Tongue.

Long before the house was finished, the workers had paid their taxes and therefore did not need any more money. We learned, however, that they would work for cloth or clothing which they did need to replace their tree-bark covering. So Herman and I went into the bartering business on a big scale. We exchanged cloth, even my draperies and all the clothes we no longer needed, for labor.

When the cloth and discarded clothing were gone, I gave out my dresses one by one, insisting, "This one does not fit very well," or "I never have liked this one." Each statement contained an element of truth—at least one percent!

Herman's wardrobe suffered, too. He consoled himself by declaring in a loud voice, "These shorts are too short," or "This shirt is too small in the collar." By the time the building was a house, all our cloth was gone except a few dress-lengths and a bolt of cream-colored curtain material so porous not even a native would feel properly dressed in it.

The house was just beginning to look like it would soon be ready when Acid-Tongue's mother-in-law died and he stopped work for several days—whether in joy or sorrow I do not know. Other days he sent the workers home for no known reason.

As the house neared completion, only two men in the district would work with Acid-Tongue—Taman Bulan, Acid-Tongue's brother-in-law, who was so slow that we nicknamed him "Slowpoke" and Ujau, a tiny, wizened fellow we affectionately called "Grandpop."

Every day the house was in process Herman spent hours checking up on the work and workers. He also had no doubt that the men accomplished more work if Tuan was present. Seldom was he pleased with what he had seen. I could usually read the events of the day on his face.

One late afternoon, when our labors were ended for the day, we walked together through the village to the riverbank facing our house and gazed across with longing eyes to the place where we hoped to live some day. We felt like

Moses viewing the promised land from Mt. Nebo.

Once a week I would go across the river with Herman and walk around our land with him while he showed me where the garden would be and the chicken house, the rice house and the house we wanted to erect for the four native boys we hoped to support while they attended public school.

Eight and a half months of work and the pattern still showed incompleteness. My husband and I decided to take a firm hand. We set a date, a Tuesday, to move into the house whether it was ready or not.

Moving day will forever be headlined in my memory as a mixture of hard work and fun. Herman and I went through the many lockers, boxes and crates while the paddlers stood by to kill the dislodged cockroaches, lizards, centipedes, spiders and rats. I packed a locker with dishes and perched it on top of a high box for lack of space. Along came Kurung and knocked it to the floor, where it landed with a thud and the telltale crack of dishes.

A *prau* transport arriving from Tandjong Selor disrupted our morning's work. On it was a five-gallon tin of nails and coffee beans. John Van Patter, kind and thoughtful as usual, wanted to send us some coffee from his trees. He conceived the idea of placing layers of papers on top of the half-tin of nails and filling the tin full of coffee beans. It was a fine idea, but the nails did not stay on the bottom and neither did the coffee stay on top. Consequently, when I should have been packing, I sat on the floor of the veranda with the men and picked nails out of coffee.

By mid-afternoon on the Tuesday the resthouse was empty. The paddlers and Kurung were at the new house when Herman and I made the last survey to see that nothing had been forgotten. Nothing but my dresses! They still hung on their line stretched across a corner of our bedroom.

"Now what do I do?" I asked myself. Not a trunk, suitcase or box remained.

I made a bundle of the dresses and wrapped them in my raincape. Now we were ready. Herman, swinging Orphan, our grey-white kitten, in her basket, and I, carrying my bundle of clothes, left the rest house for the last time.

By nightfall we felt at home. Herman and I bathed. Wearing pajamas and robes, we opened a can of vegetables and another of meat and ate dinner—just the two of us together, the world far away, our home an island of intimacy without doors, window panes or steps.

Then, the clearing of throats, knocking at our door frame and shadowy forms on our porch announced the second *prau* transport's arrival, bringing us mail that had left Tangjong Selor more than 100 days earlier.

That evening of Tuesday, October 10th, my husband and I sat on wicker chairs in a living room practically devoid of furniture and happily read letters from home postmarked in June. What a benediction to the day!

It was another couple of weeks later when we told the carpenters their work was done. The building was definitely the rough-lodge type, but it had doors—some of them hanging backward—and glass—albeit some faulty and incomplete panes.

Where the carpenters left off, Herman began. He filled knot holes in walls and floors and cracks and ill-fitting window frames. A lovely coffee table made by soldier friends huddled with three wicker chairs (the fourth lay at the bottom of the Kayan River). With a larger house, we now needed more furniture, especially cupboards and tables.

And, as had the house, so the furniture began as parasite-enshrouded trees in the jungle. Herman could see nothing wrong with the interior of the house as it was. He had a place to sleep, to eat, to bathe and to sit. It was to please me that he took on furniture making.

He scoured the village for every piece of spare lumber, and Grandpop and Slowpoke carried it to our house. They continued to work for us—that is, they worked whenever they could spare time from their mourning and hollowing-out-logs-for-coffins duties. They were in great demand when it came to hollowing out logs for coffins. And they not only faithfully observed the mourning days for their own relatives down to the 52nd cousin, but they entered into the mourning of all other families provided free food was served to the mourners. That was a district-wide custom—a custom that drew natives from the farthest corner of the surrounding jungle.

After observing Grandpop and Slowpoke at their coffin-market labors one day, I went home and wrote what I had seen and heard.

> *This morning sobbing gongs intermingled and twisted in incessant crescendo and decrescendo with sorrow-torn voices wailing "a-a-a-a-h-h-h-hu-hu-hu-hu-huuuuu, eh eh eh eh ehhhhhhhhh." A Christian mother died last evening.*
>
> *As I walked along the veranda I met two loincloth-clad boys, each carrying two headless chickens, dripping blood. Shyly the boys gazed at me. In response to my questions they told me they were on their way to the river to clean the chickens.*
>
> *Farther on, I came to a group of women beating out rice. The younger women stood on mortars which were squared-off logs with deep, scooped-out pockets in the top to hold the rice while it was beaten by women-driven pestles. Older women stood nearby winnowing the rice.*
>
> *Acknowledging the women in passing, then a group of old men sitting around a firebox feeding the fire which would later cook the chickens and rice, I opened a door on my left and stepped into a tiny, darkish room. I nodded but no one paid undue attention to me. To them I was just another mourner come to join them in their sorrow.*
>
> *Their black hair, brown eyes, tan skin and dress differed from my light hair and eyes, my blue dress and shoes. But their hearts and mine felt the same grief.*

Someone reached out to a gong leaning against the wall and placed it flat on the floor. Wordlessly he motioned for me to sit on it.

I became another link in the chain of mourners around the little mother who had died of dysentery. She lay on the floor in the center of the room, a red plaid cloth her shroud, her face uncovered, her straw hat pulling her hair back from her high forehead.

Her children, seated so as to encircle the upper part of her body, fondled her face, weeping and repeating, "We can't live without you, Mother." Calmly the mother slept, peacefully retaining a rugged beauty death could not touch.

After I had sat with the family and friends for some time, I slipped quietly out of the room, closed the door softly and turned toward the end of the veranda opposite from where I had entered. Grandpop and Slowpoke were busy fashioning a cross. On the ground at the foot of the steps eight men chopped and hewed a section of log, making a lid for the coffin which was standing ready to be carried to the room I had left a few minutes before.

That day, while sitting beside the body of my dead friend, the smouldering anger stemming from the shabby treatment meted out to our Apo Kayan people burst into full bloom. This dear lady did not have to die. Medicines were available—but not for the people of the Apo Kayan. We gave what we could, but we didn't have nearly enough to meet the need.

Thankfully though, only her body had given up its breath. Spiritually this dear native woman was alive and with Christ. That message we also had given. It was life-giving and it was enough.

14

Off to Conference

This truly is a jungle letter, coming to you from a bivouac perched precariously on the steep bank of the Kayan River. A mighty rapid roars and fights at our feet. We are tightly hugged by mountains that are practically perpendicular, their jungle-tangled mass going up and up to support a tiny canopy of hot sky over our heads. How did we get here?

Well, 20 days ago we left the last village in the Apo Kayan and have not come to another. During the 20 days we have shot rapids, we have walked, we have huddled under a tarpaulin stretched over a framework of poles while we watched the river rise and rise until we dared not launch the canoes.

Each time the river began to recede we watched some more for fear it would rise again, which it often did—then the watching and huddling started all over again. Whenever we have traveled, though, we have traveled fast. The rapids have no slow speed, neither is there any stopping unless one hits a boulder, then he stops permanently, in a grave, thus adding another cross to those already keeping guard over the rapids.

Feeling that the hardships of this trip may kill us before we arrive at Tandjong Selor, it would be easy to go on and on about the jeopardy of the journey, includ-

ing an account of the terror, weariness, discouragement, illness and hunger. But we refuse to indulge our feelings.

Herman and I had long desired to visit the villages in the lower section of the Apo Kayan. It was more than a year before we were able to arrange such an itinerary.

That fall our Mission called all missionaries in Indonesia to a conference at Benteng Tinggi, or "High Fort," our hill station near Makassar. If we left home in January, we decided, we should have time to call at each of the 13 villages and still reach Makassar in time for the conference.

The plane was in Java in the process of being repaired and would not be ready until June. Therefore we had two choices: we could choose not to attend conference or we could travel to the coast by shooting the rapids or by crossing the Apo Napo Mountain. We decided that we should attend conference (all missionaries were expected to be there) but postponed the decision about how we would get there.

If sufficient rice could be collected for a round-trip to Tandjong Selor, Mr. Soselisa would send a transport downstream in February. That would be ideal for us. We would simply join the fleet of *praus* and travel in convoy as required by law.

The weak spot in this arrangement was in the scarcity of rice in the district. The new crop was not ready to be harvested and many rice houses were almost depleted of last year's crop. If the transport was delayed we would have to go via the Apo Napo.

Since Mr. Soselisa could promise nothing, we decided to leave Long Nawang early in January and begin our village itinerary while he dealt with the rice problem. Somewhere along the way he would reach us by letter. The next few weeks would find us playing tag with the Kayan River, dashing off to the right and to the left to visit villages, but always returning to the Kayan.

I dreaded the thought of preparing for the trip. For our Borneo jungle itinerary we would need everything required for living. Outside Borneo we would want good clothes and, we hoped, nothing else except money. Experience had taught us that suitcases and trunks do not take kindly to *prau* travel. So we faced a major problem to protect them on such an extended and watery trip. Yet, we could hardly expect to take our tin-can containers aboard airplanes and ships, our means of transportation once we left Borneo to go to Makassar.

One of the national workers solved our predicament. In December he would leave Long Nawang to return to Makassar to finish his schooling. The plan was for him to take our conventional luggage part way down the river where a village chief would store it until we came.

Our first task, therefore, was to pack for the last part of our trip. Not wanting to dress too much better than the locals, we had not worn our "dressy" clothes since we left Tandjong Selor. But in the meantime, Herman's white suits and shirts had turned yellow. In fact, every article of clothing, so carefully packed away, had to be rejuvenated.

I made myself some dresses from pieces of cloth I had so tenaciously clung to while our house was being built. I ripped out zippers from old garments to put into new ones, cut up a dress to make trimming, dyed accessories and put it all together during odd moments I could find now and then.

With our "outside world" clothing stored in plastic-lined suitcases and small trunks, we turned our attention to broken-down equipment we wanted to have repaired. My typewriter had a broken carriage. The radio had not worked for months. A lantern would not burn.

Preparations for our village itinerary were vastly different. We packed all of our canned food which we had hoarded for months. We knew at least half of our days would find us eating lunch on a sandbar or rock ledge along the river. Without tins to open, such meals would consist of rice alone. That I could not face.

Besides food, there was the standard equipment: cots, bedding, lanterns and oil, gun, canteens, folding table and chairs, cooking and eating utensils and, perhaps most important, a kettle in which to boil drinking water. And we could not forget matches, soap, dishcloths, clothesline and medicine, including my precious Dramamine. While in the midst of packing these "bare necessities" a wonderful thing happened: A complete Christmas dinner in cans arrived via *prau* transport from the Van Patters, Miss Jaffray and Miss LeRoy at Long Bia. We could hardly believe our eyes.

Then there was the house to think of. Although now in our new home, for the first time in our Borneo life we felt fairly sure some of our rooms were rat proof. Still, I packed all the curtains, cushions, linens and clothing into cupboards and drums. We did not want a repeat of some of our earlier homecomings when we found remnants of curtains lying in heaps on the floor (having been eaten off their rods by rats) and mattresses and pillows with tunnels through them. In fact, every article not made of aluminum had been attacked by some sort of animal—and the aluminum corroded.

In the Apo Kayan everybody knows what everybody else is doing. The whole district knew almost as soon as we did that Tuan and Nyonya were leaving and would not return for an indefinite period. As the date of our departure pressed us to frenzied activity, a continuous line of people filed into the house. They came to bid us farewell, to stare and to generally get in our way.

At the first suggestion of a new day, while we were eating breakfast, we heard the ominous scraping-over-stones noise of a large *prau* being poled upstream. This *prau*, huge in size and usually used only for racing, ornately decorated and intricately carved, beached on our sandbar and 16 men stepped out.

"We came early to help Tuan and Nyonya get ready," a big, handsome, middle-aged Kenya informed us.

When Herman reminded the men that we had arranged for a smaller *prau* and fewer men, the Kenya answered, "Yes, but we want to take our father and mother to Long Jelerai for, who knows, perhaps we shall never see our father and mother again and we want to show that we love them."

What could we do but accept their offer graciously, although I did feel my graciousness strained at times by the dubious help they gave us.

Although the *prau* was practically empty of luggage, I was granted no choice as to where I wished to sit. That was arranged before I appeared on the scene. The paddlers had chosen the center of the *prau* and dedicated it to us. They had lined a space with a lovely mat, placed our bed roll for a backRest and roofed that portion of the *prau* with pandanus leaves.

Herman had seen to it that a handful of bananas, a thermos of coffee, drinking water, his shotgun and my handbag were arranged conveniently nearby.

We were off! But not really. Our house was located at the upper end of the village which meant that we had to pass by the main section of the village before heading downriver.

First we stopped to say goodbye to Lieutenant Gaillard and our soldier friends who waited on their bank of the river. Next we crossed to the village side where we shook hands with seemingly countless people, saying a few words to each. Then in God's magnificent outdoor cathedral, roofed by His heavens, walled by His mountains and carpeted by His earth and river, we bowed our heads and Herman led us in prayer, requesting God to watch over us all during our separation.

As I stepped toward the *prau* a woman blocked my pathway. In her hand was a chunk of venison, still dripping blood. Kurung came and relieved me of it. We took our places in the *prau* and pulled away from the sandbar.

Everyone waved. I jerked my handkerchief out of my pocket and as I did, my sunglasses came too. They flew into the river. I had no others, so we simply had to find them. Several boys dived, came up for air and dived again and again until one of them came up with the glasses. Herman gave him the only piece of money he had in his pocket.

We started again. As we drifted away from our friends we felt sad. We knew Long Nawang would not be the same upon our return or ever again. Lieutenant Gaillard was going to Holland, the army was leaving the village and the Soselisas were being transferred to another island.

Taman Ringget was headman of the *prau*. In his younger days Taman had been considered the strongest and most clever paddler in the Apo Kayan. But now he was old. He sat in front of us and held no paddle in his hand. He swayed with those doing the rhythm paddling. And when he turned to talk with us he stretched out his hand to the side of the *prau* to steady himself. The tatoo, "Christian man," stood out in blue on his arm. He told us that his eyes had been badly burned by gunpowder some years before and that they still hurt him. "Would his mother and father (us) please buy him glasses in Makassar?"

"Yes," we said, "we will." And we did.

Arriving at Long Jelerai, the first village of the 13, we saw no visible signs of preparation for our arrival, despite the fact that the people had known for weeks that we would arrive on that day. The *kubu* was filthy. Refuse left by human beings, dogs and chickens blanketed the floor. I philosophically accepted the fact that we must bow to the native custom never to prepare a room for a guest until he or she arrived. *Why go to all the trouble of sweeping the floor before a visitor comes?* they reasoned. *Something might happen to prevent his arrival and then all that energy would be wasted!*

I do not know whether dramamine or just plain fatigue sent me to my cot to sleep away the whole afternoon. Whatever the cause, as soon as Taman Ringget and his party ate lunch, said good-bye and were waved off, I flung myself down and was sound asleep by the time I finished thinking, *If anyone needs me he will call.*

By late afternoon, when seven natives from beyond the Apo Napo Mountain moved in with us, I was awake and up. We felt crowded that night, but nothing like we felt the following evening when 20 Kayans came to spend the night. We held several church services, including baptismal and communion, after which we did our best to ease the sufferings of the sick.

My acquaintance with our titanic *prau*, which I christened "The Rolling Stone," began the morning we left Long Jelerai for Marong, our second stop. Herman planned to use this mammoth *prau* on the deep Kayan River and change to smaller craft for our side expeditions.

The trip down the secondary river was fast and easy. I enjoyed the lovely patterns woven by gaudy butterflies and pert kingfishers on the jungle-green background. Sometimes the second canoe darted ahead of ours and sometimes it lagged behind, depending on when the men cast their nets into likely spots for fish.

At noon I took note of our sandbar dining room. In front of us a tablecloth was spread on the ground, complete with stainless steel silverware and enamel plates. We ate our rice, tuna and Christmas dinner with forks and drank steaming coffee from the thermos.

Nearby the men squatted on the ground and ate from a mound of boiled cassava seasoned with a few tiny, bony fish. And they endured a severe attack of the fidgets waiting for Kurung to wash, scald and pack our utensils. They could not understand why Nyonya insisted that they all be locked inside *bliks*. Did not lids and frying pans make excellent dippers for bailing water from the *praus*? As for me, I refused to use a frying pan or any other utensil after it had been used to bail out *praus* of feet-washings, spittle and worse.

Leaving Marong and arriving back down at the Kayan River, we found The Rolling Stone where we had left it. I was glad we could transfer to a comfortable seat for the rest of the trip down the wide Kayan.

The following morning we said a regretful good-bye to some of our helpers. During the few days we had known them we had learned to love them. It had been fun traveling under their care.

By 10 o'clock that night we had reached our *kubu*. This one had not been cleaned either. So, while a number of boys stirred up the stale dust on the floor with bunches of leaves and a hundred or so natives looked on with lively curiosity, we made camp. I was tired, too tired to care if the whole population watched while the first white lady to visit their village undressed, bathed in the river, ate her supper and crawled into bed.

Neither did I care that they crowded around my cot and noisily took turns peeping inside my mosquito net. I calmly went to sleep and left them staring. I am not sure whether they stayed there all night, but I do know that they—or some just like them—were there when I opened my eyes the next morning.

It was late afternoon when we sighted the next village. The first thing we saw was a tiny, brown something built high over the river. My suspicions were soon confirmed—it was a specially-made latrine for my use. Pandanus-leaf-walls on three sides, the river side open (most of the traffic was on that side), a hole in the unsteady floor, the river swirling underneath—and the lady's private toilet was ready!

At the chief's home, cockroaches scurried from the two decorative mats unrolled for us. We sat and immediately took up our role as guests by seeking information. How is your rice crop this year? Is there much sickness in the village?

Meanwhile, the chief's beaming wife fulfilled her obligation as hostess by placing trays of bananas in front of us and by serving *semangka*, a pale, tasteless version of watermelon. Using the never-scrubbed floor as a chopping block, she hacked the *semangka* to pieces with a headhunting knife that had cut everything from toenails to heads.

Rooms in longhouses are always crowded. We found our room a bit crowded with the regular inhabitants—the chief and his wife, their granddaughter, her husband and two children, Kurung, a schoolboy named Lawai, 10 cats, several birds in cages and any number of dogs that could slip in from the veranda. In addition the room contained any and all of the 240 villagers who came to visit with Tuan and Nyonya or simply to sit and watch them eat, sleep or dress.

When Chief Pelibut lay down on his mat instead of giving one of his much-loved and well-executed oratorical speeches of welcome, we knew he was a sick man. According to him, he would die just any moment. In fact, his coffin had been prepared and stored beneath the house. And, judging by appearances, he was indeed hovering near death.

With my social amenities paid to the other folks, I went over to the old chief, sat on the floor beside him and began to poke his skinny body in an effort to locate his pain. As I did so I smiled to think of my manhandling an old headhunter. I wonder what he thought when he found himself helpless in the hands of a woman!

Then, kneeling beside him, Herman and I prayed that he would get well again. I fed him pills every two hours and with every dose I told him, "You are going to get well. This is the best medicine in the world for your sickness."

We knew he was feeling better when he told us that he did not think the coffin would be used for some time to come. And, before we left, the aged, wrinkled and shrunken—but still fiery—chief found strength to give in part, at least, the speech he was unable to give when we arrived.

Herman in his response acknowledged every one of the 240 villagers as our children and assured them that their father and mother would not stay away longer than absolutely necessary and that we appreciated but did not need their gifts. Just to be with them made us happy.

Church services at this village were typical of all the services we conducted in other villages. They began early in the morning and were conducted on the veranda in front of the chief's room. Herman and I sat on a mat-draped bench, facing bright sunlight and the audience who were seated on the floor with their backs to the open side of the veranda.

As Herman preached, chickens clucked and sang in their baskets hanging around the edge of the veranda. Dogs howled their protest at being kicked aside. Mothers, with babies in carrying baskets on their backs, stood just outside the seated congregation, jiggling back and forth in perfect rhythm: lean forward, two jiggles; straighten up, one jiggle; and then forward to the two jiggles.

Again the boom of gongs rang through the village calling everyone to come say good-bye to Tuan and Nyonya. From the time we stepped out of the chief's door until we reached the *prau*, we shook hands along the people-lined pathway. Then, until a bend in the river came between us, we waved our handkerchiefs and they waved a part of some garment or leaves. (My private toilet was dismantled to supply the leaves! Why not? It would not be used until Nyonya came again and it would not be much work to build her another one.)

That night we arrived at Data Dian. One year before, when I came to the village from the outside world, mountains crowding in on all sides made it very difficult for Al Lewis to land our small Beechcraft. Now, after living at Long Nawang, where mountains all but rubbed our noses, Data Dian seemed to rest in a spacious valley.

Herman, ever thoughtful of me, suggested that we spend a few extra days at Data Dian. We were given a room in the pastor's house and, with the door shut, I felt comfortably private although I knew everyone passing the door took a peep over the top to see what was going on inside.

I was tired. As much as I hated to say it, I had to admit that those black smudges around my eyes might be caused by weariness. Our schedule had been a heavy one. Battling through rapids, living in longhouses, being on constant display, conducting church services and taking care of the sick—all had drained any reserve of strength I might have possessed.

Moreover, I was traveling more hours than anyone else in the party. During the days, the men and Herman joined me in the motion of the *praus*—jerk, roll, roll; jerk, roll, roll; jerk, roll, roll. At night the men went to sleep. But when I laid on my cot with my eyes closed, I repeated every jerk and roll of the day—the only difference being that I now lay flat on my back.

Then as the motion gradually ceased, I would drift into an uneasy slumber where I cleaned ulcers, dressed wounds, distributed quinine, salts and castor oil, dropped medicine into sore and sometimes blind eyes.

At Kayan Pura I was asked to visit a man who was reported to be too badly wounded to come to me.

"Where is his wound?" I asked.

"His head. A tree fell on it."

"Is it a new wound?" I continued, trying to determine what sort of drugs to take along.

"Fairly new. Two or three months," came the answer.

"Well, is it a clean wound or is there pus?"

"Lots of pus."

"Say, dear," I called to Herman, "will you go with me to see a man with a cracked head?"

A "cracked head" was an understatement. When I lifted the dirty rag covering his head I almost fainted. A great tear jagged across his head, with the front of his skull pushed lower than the top of his head. Such quantities of puss boiled in the gaping wound that I could not tell by mere sight whether it was all infection or a mixture of pus and brains. It must have been pure infection, for I washed it all away and, so far as I could see, he still retained his full quota of brains.

One day, a year later, I came home from teaching my classes. When I walked onto our veranda my husband pointed to one of the several men sitting on the floor.

"Here is a friend of yours," he said.

I recognized the man by the dent in his head, now perfectly healed to a scar. He thanked us for "healing" him.

Back to the Kayan River. Darkness was turning the village as black as the surrounding jungle as we beached our *praus* in front of the chief's house.

"Can't we stay in the *kubu* this one night?" I pleaded with Herman. "I simply cannot stand another crowd staring at me right now."

"Where is the *kubu*?" my husband shouted to the people collecting on the shore.

"There is no *kubu*. You are to stay in the chief's house."

Huge tears rolled down my face. I could not face a dark, windowless room full of people inside a longhouse. But, I did. And no one knew of the tears except my husband.

We arrived next at Chief Pelisa Lendjau's village. I knew Chief Pelisa to be a fine Christian gentleman. It was common knowledge, however, that the chief had served a long prison term for "cutting heads." I wished to hear the story from his own lips and was determined to do so, but fear kept me from asking outright whether he really had been a head-hunter.

My chance came one evening when I found the old man squatting in regal splendor on his shiny brass gong beside his fireplace. I sat on the floor by his side while we gossiped about trivialities and smoke writhed to the rafters and dogs hugged the fire as well as our feet for warmth. When I thought I was on safe ground, I asked, "Chief, where did you learn to speak such excellent Indonesian?"

A knowing twinkle brightened his faded eyes and a smile creased his face.

"Nyonya," he responded, "while I was still a very young chief, I cut heads. Of course, in doing so I merely followed the custom of my tribe." Then quickly he added, "Since that time we have cut no more heads."

According to Chief Pelisa, many years earlier some Kayans stole into his territory and "cut four heads." "We could do nothing right then in retaliation," reminisced the chief, "for our rice crops were ready to harvest. Consequently we could not leave home."

When the rice had been stored, Pelisa Lendjau organized a punitive expedition of nine men plus himself. Spending a few night hours in Kayan land, they brought home 10 Kayan heads.

"Nyonya, what a pity we did not know that Dutch troops and a representative of the government had moved to Long Nawang while we harvested our rice."

"Would your knowing have made a difference?" I asked.

"Yes, had we known," the chief responded, "we would have been more careful."

Hints of the "taking of 10 heads" reached government ears. Police officers were sent to investigate. The guilty were apprehended and questioned. They were convinced that the officers wanted only to see the heads. Not understanding exactly how or why the government would be interested, Pelisa led the officers to the hidden heads. Each of the 10 men was given a prison sentence, but Pelisa Lendjau, the leader, drew a 10-year term. "One year for each head," Chief Pelisa recalled.

"Had I been content to take those 10 heads one by one over a long period I could have gotten away with it. But 10 heads in one night were nine too many!"

Herman was every bit as tired as I was. The burden of the trip had been his. He had done the preaching and had spent endless hours helping the Christians solve their problems. And he had supervised the loading and unloading of the *praus*.

Whenever possible he had helped me with the sick. With unfailing courtesy he had assisted me into and out of *praus*, proudly introduced me to each congregation and treated me with such kind respect that the natives in every village marveled at the high esteem an American man holds for a woman.

He had given me the best place to sit in the *praus* and the cot the farthest away from people in the longhouses. At night he had let me rest while he flung firewood at dogs to keep them from eating our supplies.

Surrounded by sickness and disease, I had often looked across a milling mob to my husband's smile. And my world had slipped back into focus. Just the two of us—and our God—in a world far from our own.

15

Shooting "Big" Rapids

We followed a heavy schedule—a day tossing all over the river in a canoe, with a service in the evening. The next day full of services—the earliest began at 9 a.m., the latest at 10 p.m. Then, another day in canoes, with the evening and following day services as usual. Thus, it continued until we had visited 13 villages. Herman, aided by the national workers, baptized 627 precious Dyaks, most of whom had been waiting long for our coming.

One Sunday, Herman and Markus baptized 111 people and then gave communion to 246, using only eight glasses. (We aimed to bring more from America but many were broken.) In addition to the baptisms and communion services, the gospel was preached to huge crowds while almost the entire population received what medical help we could give them. By the time we came to Long Heban, the last village, our medicine, pictures, cloth, used clothing and food were gone. Our bodies were exhausted too, but that could not keep us from praising God for giving us such a good itinerary.

God faithfully watched over us during the 24 days

en route from Long Heban to Tandjong Selor. Imagine taking 24 days to make a trip that can be done in one hour by plane!

We waited all day Wednesday in Data Dian, but the transport Mr. Soselisa was supposed to send to meet us did not come. Neither did it come on Thursday, Friday, Saturday or Sunday. What could we do? Our *praus* and crews had left. We were stuck—Herman, Kurung and I—unable to go upstream or down.

Perhaps the paddlers had struck for higher pay before they would leave Long Nawang or perhaps the paddlers from Long Ban were holding up the transport or perhaps they could not get enough rice for the trip. Maybe it wasn't coming at all.

Meanwhile, we waited out the days and nights in the *kubu*. Dried fish turned and turned as it hung from a rafter. Chickens cackled and fought in baskets over by the wall. The fire smoked while the wind from the river blew it into our faces. Dogs fought under the *kubu*, around the *kubu* and inside the *kubu*. Hogs grunted in the same places and followed us like a pack of dogs every time we stepped outside the building. People came from far and near for medicine and just to talk. Each evening we conducted a service.

One morning I was sitting on my folding chair at our folding table writing the notes that form the basis of this book. A group of children was sitting off to one side watching me. Herman was reading nearby. The early morning sun had reached the tops of the surrounding mountains but had not found its way down to where we were. That would come about noon.

A little way off, the part of a longhouse that a fire had left was being torn down accompanied by much noise and confusion. Suddenly every sound ceased. The place became so quiet it seemed we were sitting in a vacuum. Then a man came running.

"A beam fell on a man's head. He's bleeding all over," he blurted.

Grabbing up our medicine kit, we made a dash down the ladder, across the narrow foot log crossing a stream, up the other side and then up another ladder to where we saw a crowd of people. The wounded man was sitting there looking very pale and bloody. The crowd was pressing in on him.

The beam had fallen from the top of the house, hitting him on the back of the head and cutting two deep gashes. That had knocked him forward and he hit his forehead on a rock which had cut another gash. The forehead was easy, but before we could touch the back of his head his long black hair had to be cut.

We finally got the wounds clean and filled them with sulfanilamide crystals and covered them with gauze.

"Now fix a mat for him," I ordered. We left the wounded man feeling drowsy but comfortable. "Now don't move him today. Let him lie there and sleep," we told the family.

Herman and I returned to the *kubu* and again took up our reading and writing. Soon a runner came.

"The man is bleeding again."

This time we found the man sitting on a chair, ready to faint. A tent had been made over and around him and huge pots of boiling water placed under his chair and around him inside the tent, causing blood to flow from every wound.

"Why did you do that?" Herman demanded, pointing to the half-cooked man.

"To make him hot so his blood would flow again," they answered as though this were the common practice. It was.

Of course the adhesive tape had let go, allowing the bandages to slip. The people had tied a piece of dirty tree bark around his head. What could we do? The white man's cures were one thing—the customs of centuries another. We weren't in town long enough to find out how the man really fared.

Finally, after seven days, four of the *praus* that were to make up the transport arrived. The others would be down right away, they said. We waited some more. Each day our food became less and less and we became more worried about the trip downstream. Fortunately, we were able to buy chickens and rice, and we still had oatmeal for Herman's breakfast and coffee for both of us.

Then the Kayan River flooded and no one could travel. More long frustrating days.

"Why don't we take two *praus* and go on down to Busang Tengah?" Herman asked Buwan, the head of the *praus*. "If we take 16 paddlers we will have enough to portage our luggage the 18 miles to the lower end of the big rapids. We can save time."

Although time was not really something the people of the Apo Kayan worried about too much, Buwan said, "All right. Tonight I will talk it over with the others and let you know whether we can leave tomorrow or not."

We packed. We waited for word, but heard nothing. We decided the *prau*-men must have decided not to leave the following day. But before we were out of bed the next morning, someone came.

"We are leaving this morning," the courier announced. Everyone scurried to get ready as quickly as possible. By 8 o'clock we were ready and sitting on top of our piled-up baggage. At 10:30 we were still sitting there.

"All right," said Buwan, "we're ready to start." That was good, for even I could see that the two *praus* were overloaded. Now that we had collected all our belongings, I instructed the crew, "Be sure to pack the suitcases so they can't get wet."

The people stood on the beach as the two *praus* slowly drifted away from them. The men maneuvered them out into the current. We waved, and the people waved, shouted goodbyes and sang until a bend in the river separated us. When the villagers were no longer in view, Herman and I rearranged our seats, grinned at each other and said, "Now we're really off."

But no sooner had we said that than the crew proved us wrong. We stopped at every shack in every rice field to pick up rice or bananas, once to cook and eat lunch, sometimes just to visit. By night we were barely out of sight of Long Heban's longhouses.

The second *prau* went ahead, and by the time we arrived at the camping site our shelter was up. We were grateful for that unusual blessing. It was also a relief to have no more that 17 people watching our every move.

After supper there was nothing to do. We could hardly believe it—nothing to do! We had been living the life of an animal in a zoo for so long that now, more or less by ourselves, our nerves relaxed and our bodies felt like they were dropping into little pieces. It was good to stretch out on our cots, watch the flickering fires with the *prau*-men and Kurung lazing around them and listen to a spurt of chatter, then quietness when the song of the jungle took over.

It was peaceful here. I would float away on the peacefulness only to be suddenly snatched

SHOOTING "BIG" RAPIDS

back to reality by the thought of what we were to face on the morrow. Buwan had told us that tomorrow we would enter the "real" rapids.

Real rapids! What were those we had gone through up the other river? I didn't want to see any that were more real. Even then, lying on my cot, I could hear the roar of the one we had shot just before making camp. That was real, wasn't it?

Having expressed something of this to Buwan earlier in the evening, he had told me, "Yes, these are 'real' rapids. But if anyone dies in them, it is because he is careless," implying that if we died in the ones scheduled for the morrow it might not be our fault. Recalling the names of the rapids, for each had a name with meaning, I wondered what our future was to be.

Early the next morning, before daybreak, we were up. If we had to shoot rapids, let's shoot them and get it over with!

We ate breakfast. We packed. We sat. The men ate, squatted at the edge of the river and smoked and talked.

Finally Herman asked, "Are we starting today or not?"

"Don't know, Tuan," answered Buwan. "The third *prau* has not come. It was supposed to meet us here."

"Why didn't you tell us before we packed?" Herman asked somewhat angrily.

No answer—true to Kenya style.

We sat on stones and waited until 10:30. Then Buwan, flanked by some reinforcements, sidled up to us and squatted on his heels. After clearing his throat several times, he began. "Perhaps we should start. It doesn't look like the other *prau* is coming."

At 11 o'clock the paddlers picked up their paddles and we pulled away from shore. Hardly had we entered the *prau* when the rain began to fall like great giants were swishing water over us from great buckets. But we had to go on—there was no place to stop. In midafternoon we shot out of a dark tunnel of water into bright sunshine.

It wasn't long until we arrived at the first "real" rapids, and we began our first portage. Herman and I scrambled over huge boulders along the edge of the river while the men skillfuly lowered the *prau* by tying strong rattan ropes to both stern and bow and easing it along the bank.

Standing high on top of a boulder, I could feel my body tighten as the men hung onto those ropes for dear life. And by the time we were to a safe place I felt like doing just what the crew was doing—falling flat on the shore to get my breath. They had carried the cargo around the rapids. Then they had portaged the *prau* itself. Herman and I had maneuvered the same slippery, moss-covered boulders free of baggage.

No sooner had we started down the river than Buwan got out and examined the height of the river and looked over a large rapid that loomed downstream.

"We can shoot this one," he finally said. The men picked up their paddles and pulled into the current, heading straight for the scattered boulders. It seemed impossible not to hit at least one. *They can't hope to miss them all, and the first crash will be our last,* I thought to myself.

With lacy foam in my face and upon every impact of the waves on the bow of the *prau*, fear slapped me in the face and spread to my entire body. It was beyond my will. I could do nothing about it.

I marveled at our crew. Before approaching the rapid, they were individuals. But once committed to the rapid they became one, a poem of rhythm, following the leader who stood in the front of the *prau*. He stood—they all stood. He shouted—every man with perfect timing dug in with his paddle. There were not eight men, but one. Not eight paddles, but one.

Soon we pulled up to a wide sandy beach where Buwan said we were to spend the night. We saw a cross. That meant a soldier had drowned there.

Rain poured all the time camp was being made. While the men put up poles and erected the tent, I stood around trying to share my umbrella with a piece of luggage. I was longing for the time when I could crawl into the tent and change into dry clothes. But when the tent was up, rain poured inside almost as much as outside, the only difference being that outside the drops were large and came straight down. Inside, they sprayed, having hit the canvas first.

While Herman and I arranged the interior, the men were busy erecting a lean-to for themselves and Kurung was cooking our supper, stirring the pot with one hand and holding the umbrella with the other. We were wet and cold and the sun—even if it did come out—would not reach us even in mid-afternoon because of the narrowness of the gorge. The hot coffee helped. We didn't dare open our *bliks* because of the driving rain. It seemed that our beds would be the only dry place.

Rain poured all night, plopping on the canvas, a fine spray falling on us. When we awoke, there was no world, only a mass of wet grey mist. However, by the time we had eaten breakfast the world was coming into being— the jungle back of us, sand underneath, trees overhead.

"Let's carry this stuff to the canoes," Buwan called to the paddlers. I went along with the last load just to check the suitcases which, it turned out, had gotten wet in the night in spite of the fact that we had covered them with large leaves.

"Tuan," I heard Buwan saying to Herman, "we are afraid to start because the river is rising." It was obvious that the river was coming up fast. Even we knew there was nothing to do but wait. One learns to wait in Borneo—or die.

Noon came and we unpacked enough of one *prau* to get out the cooking equipment. Then we sat down and waited some more. I had my eye on a rock out in the stream. It would be nice to wade out to it, using it as a perch to survey the gorge. But as the water level rose on it, my heart sank. If we went for a walk, the only place we could go would be to the soldier's grave. Not a happy thought.

Late in the afternoon, too late to move, the water began to inch down. We went to bed in high spirits. Tomorrow early we would be on our way.

Not so. Next morning the river was higher than it had been the day before. So we sat another day, leaving the dubious shelter of our tent every once in a while to see how the soldier's grave was getting along.

At dawn, following the third night, I sat up in bed, took a look at the river and saw nothing encouraging. The Kayan was every bit as high as the day before and higher than it had been the first day of our stay. Facing another sandy day, I lay down again and did not get up until Kurung had coffee made. We ate breakfast, watched the water swirl, read our Bible and prayed together.

We were drinking a final cup of coffee when a spurt of activity whirled around the paddlers' lean-to.

"Herman, the men are tearing down their lean-to. Why?" I asked.

"I don't know. Hey, Buwan, what's going on?" demanded Herman.

"Better start, Tuan," said Buwan as he stopped beside our table. At the same moment the men swarmed over us like bees, picking up everything they could get their hands on and carrying it down to the *praus*.

"But Buwan," Herman continued, "the river is higher than the day before yesterday when you said it was too high." Silence. Obviously they knew more about the river than we did. Or did they?

While the *praus* were being loaded, I looked at the river, then at the *praus* then at the grave nearby. My heart tightened until it felt like stone and nerves formed a huge knot in my stomach. I walked over to the soldier's grave. As I stood there I wondered if before the end of the day Herman and I would add two more graves to the riverside. Taking a final glance upstream to see if the other *praus* were coming and finding the river empty as far as eye could see, I went back to our camp. Herman and the men were awaiting my return.

Herman helped me into the *prau* while Buwan held up the leaf shelter overhead. I tucked the thermos of coffee close by, pushed the shotgun farther away and slid over into the middle of the *prau*. With a shout we shot out into the current to begin a long day of terror. Never once were we out of sound of the roaring rapids that filled the valley, rising to the mountain tops, flinging back down on our heads. Neither were we out of sight of a rapid. Having safely traversed one, another would loom directly ahead just waiting to grab the *prau* and dash it to pieces.

There were always three choices when facing another set of rapids. The men would pull to the side of the river, tie up the *praus* and, without a word to us, leave the *prau* to go jumping from stone to stone to reach the lower level of the rapid. Then, coming back more slowly, they would study the water. By the time they reached the *prau* the decision was made. Mostly, we took off into the rapid like an express train, the current spewing the *prau* past boulder after boulder and finally into calmer water.

Or the second option was that the men would take the *prau* through but Tuan and Nyonya would have to walk. Out we would scramble, after having put on our shoes, and head up over the moss-covered stones as slippery as a skating rink. At some point the shoes would come off and we would end up crawling on our hands and knees over and around boulders some of which were as large as a five-room house.

The third option was to portage everything. When this happened I would crawl out onto a wet rock, sit with my back against the jungle and read a book until everything—*praus* and cargo—had been transported to our new launching site.

This time the decision was to portage everything a half-mile to reach a camping place. It turned out that our camping spot was surrounded by leeches. I was sitting, carefully guarding my legs from the marauders, when one of the men dropped three large tins in front of me.

"Better check these out for water," he said. "I dropped them in the river."

The first two were fine, but the third, containing my typewriter, had more than an inch of water in it. Obviously the machine would now need more repairs than we had planned on.

It was determined that we would arrive at the next village about noon the next day. The name of village was Kiham Mawon, meaning "big-waves-like-smoke-so-can't-see-beyond." It was often referred to as "the grandfather of all rapids." Here we would leave our *praus* and walk 18 miles to the lower end of the "big" rapids.

I had seen all the rapids I ever wanted to see. I didn't know if I could face the "big-waves-like-smoke-so-can't-see-beyond." I wished I didn't have to. But the world lay on the other side. I had no choice.

16

Leech Trail

January 7 to February 5, Mary and I visited the 13 villages in the lower Apo Kayan. We taught about the Lord's Supper and observed communion in 10 villages. In addition, we dedicated hundreds of children, doctored scores of sick and baptized a total of 639 converts. The greatest number of baptized in one village was 241 at Long Heban. It is the farthest village downstream from Long Nawang and badly in need of a resident worker.

March 17 we embarked for Makassar to attend field conference. While enroute, the Indonesian guilder was depreciated 50 percent of its value. Hence, we lost one half of several months' allowances which had been accummulating at Tandjong Selor while the plane was out of commission.

About 11 o'clock the next morning, for the first time since we left Long Nawang, we could not hear or see a rapid. The river widened out until it was like a glassy lake. Hemmed in by jungle, canopied by blue sky, we floated over the peaceful surface. Despite my having been warned about the "big" rapids we were nearing, I simply could not believe they could be within reach that day.

But, just around a bend in the river, there they were. The beautiful, calm lake narrowed to funnel its contents into a rock-bound vise. Here we were to leave our *praus*—no boat could live in the angry waves, I was told. I had trouble believing that. They didn't look bad to me.

Wanting to see these famous rapids for myself, I insisted that Herman go with me for a climb along the sides. We scrambled over boulders, around boulders and jumped from boulder to boulder until we were far enough downstream to look up and see the upper end of the first "big" rapid. Great black boulders reared their heads here and there in midstream, but for the most part the rapids looked like waves to me.

However, somewhere in the funnel the waves seemed to head back against themselves, and therein lay their deadliness. As far as we could see upstream and then downstream we saw the same fight-to-the-death going on. Now I understood why no boat could survive.

What grandeur! What awe! Primary jungle—so dense that the trunks of the trees could not be seen—rose to a heavenly blue canopy spread over us. The roar of the rapids filled the whole area. Herman and I looked and felt like midgets who had strayed into a garden of prehistoric monsters.

LEECH TRAIL

The next day we began the 18-mile walk commonly called Leech Trail. It was February 16. I am convinced that leech runners preceded us down the trail spreading the news that two pale faces were to pass that way and announcing that we had the best blood in the world. They were on the path, on the low bushes and on higher bushes—all aimed at various parts of our bodies. Once contact was made, the leeches hung on for dear life—green ones, black ones, brown ones—bloodsuckers all.

But leeches weren't the only delegates to this convention. Ants—black, black and red, big and little—crawled up our legs and raced up our arms. Sandflies joined them.

The paddlers had left before us. As we went on, we saw that they had not fared any better than we—we knew where the trail was by the blood spots from their leech bites. At times I felt I simply could not go down to the bottom of another ravine and, if I did, I certainly could never climb out of it. I could not bear to have my feet slip between two stones again; if another ant ran up my arm or another leech struck my legs, I was certain I would scream.

About the time my nerves were about to snap, we came in sight of the camp. We had traversed half of the trail.

Blessed crew! I loved every one of them at that moment. They had already erected our tent and were now sitting around a high mound of rice poured out onto green leaves, grinning and eating their lunch. I was too tired and my feet hurt too much to care about lunch.

When I discovered that the men had erected our tent on ground that slanted toward the river I didn't love them quite so much.

After supper—rice as usual—Herman and I took a bath in the cold mountain stream. I found a stone in the center on which to wash my hair. *Did I look anything like a mermaid?* I wondered longingly to myself.

Again the leeches swarmed our camp. I put off finding a private place in the bushes as long as possible although Herman had found what he called "a good place" for me. When nature could no longer be denied, I went.

As I stood up, I suspected that all was not well. "Herman, Herman, please come here," I called in a panic.

"Honey, what's wrong?" he shouted as he came running.

"I think one of those filthy leeches is on my behind!"

"Let's see," Herman said as he turned me around.

"He's a whopper," he finally announced, holding a large green leech up for me to see.

That night we climbed into our sloping bed.

"Herman," I called across the tent, "if I'm not here in the morning, I will have slid into the river. Look for me there."

Our clothes had not been washed for weeks. So on the morning of the second day in camp, Kurung got busy and did the laundry. I helped him hang all those clothes on lines we erected. But before they could dry out, it rained. They still were not dry when we broke camp for the next stage of the journey. I separated them out, putting those "nearly dry" in one bag, the "real wet" ones in another.

Had I known that the second half of the trail to the bottom of the rapids would be worse than the first I don't think I could have found the courage even to start. But not knowing, and being anxious to be on our way, we set out.

That day, as we walked along the trail, we continually marveled at the cleverness of our paddlers. We also had some most unkind things to say about a government that required its people to use such a trail. Neither did our Mission board escape criticism for not providing air travel. Of course, the members of that board were perfectly innocent, but they were sitting in the safety and luxury of New York while we were slipping and sliding—and not always on our feet, either—on that trail so far removed from civilization that we felt we were the only people in the world. The whole scene made fertile ground for self-pity.

The men had gone ahead and were out of sight. I came next, with Herman bringing up the rear, although there were more of the crew somewhere back on the trail. We kept following what looked like a trail, at least as much as anything we had seen that day, but we failed to see one turn.

After going some distance we sensed we were lost—no longer could we find drops of blood or footprints. Herman left me and went on ahead to investigate. Fortunately he met a Dyak out hunting.

"Yes, Tuan, you are lost," he assured Herman. While they were getting the directions straight, leeches swarmed over me and ants turned my body into a thoroughfare. I made a half-hearted swipe at them but was too tired to really attack them like they were attacking me.

I thought of my Dad saying that the people in one section of West Virginia have one leg shorter than the other from walking on the side of those hills. I believed his story. I didn't have one leg shorter, but by the end of the day I had pulled a muscle, broken the arch of my shoe and sprained my ankle. Splotches on my skin from contact with poisonous plants lasted for weeks after. We finally arrived at Busang Tengah.

The last of the crew finally arrived at camp. What had happened, I asked, to my two bags of clothes that had been packed wet several days before? The answer was that somewhere en route the two men carrying them decided that one bag was heavier than the other. So they had sat down beside the trail and divided the clothes to even out the weight. We were in great need of something clean if not entirely dry to put on, and here were our clothes—all the same wetness. By the time everything was finally dried out, we had lived a total of 11 days without dry clothes.

"Honey, do you want to go over and talk with our neighbors?" Herman asked about dark. I was lying on my cot nursing my lame leg and ankle, trying not to scratch the infection and feeling sorry for myself.

"No," I said disgustedly. About then I didn't want to go anywhere but to heaven.

"Will you be all right if I go for a few minutes?"

"Sure."

The news Herman brought back was on a par with everything else that had happened on that day. The Van Patters and children, and Miss Jaffray and Miss LeRoy had all gone to Makassar for vacation and conference. That meant that the Mission homes at Long Bia were empty. As Herman told me the news I felt hot tears stinging my eyes. Nothing during the trip had so disappointed me. I was looking forward to having our friends welcome us to clean surroundings, and most of all, to ice water! So many times during the trip I had dreamed of having some ice water!

The next morning the men were a bit apprehensive about taking off from Busang Tengah. The river was high. We did not insist. We knew that for the first half day we would be in "bad" rapids.

By mid-morning we were in a flood of no mean proportions. The good news was that we were below the "bad" rapids, considered by those who knew what they were talking about, the most dangerous. We were now at the whirlpools.

It is a tricky business maneuvering *praus* through whirlpools. The idea is to keep the *prau* on the rim of the whirlpool. If the men misjudge and get inside the whirl, the *prau* will be sucked into the funnel. It is especially tricky when the whirlpool reaches the entire width of the river.

No one had any food to speak of by now, except rice. Buwan, thinking he must do something about this, took the gun and went hunting that noon. Within a few minutes he was back with a pig.

That night we set up cots, hung up mosquito nets and spread out our wet clothing so it would not mildew and went to bed. It was pouring rain, as usual. It continued all night. By morning the river was several feet higher than it had been the day before—too high to travel. However, after lunch the crew decided that since there were no bad rapids for the next few miles we could go. A cold rain plastered our already rain-soaked clothes to our shivering bodies.

That night we stopped at a small *kubu*, the dirtiest hole on earth. Flies swarmed up from a floor that actually oozed filth. In the midst of the filth lay a man, groaning. He had been to

Tandjong Selor and had been vaccinated. The area had become infected. Now his whole upper arm was a mass of dripping pus.

We were now only one day from Long Bia and, although the folks were not there, we would be able to use their house for a day or so. We watched the river rise higher and higher. By late afternoon it was a raging torrent. That evening we were down to the very last of our food—a small tin of liver paste and rice plus enough oatmeal for one more breakfast.

That evening Buwan said to Herman, "Tuan, we paddlers from the Apo Kayan don't know this river down here very well. We are afraid. But if you will request a third *prau* so as to lighten our loads, we are willing to go on tomorrow."

That was the best news we had heard for ages. Calling the local men together, Herman got enough to promise to go. They were not afraid of the river between their village and Long Bia. They knew the way. That night we went to bed happy. The next day we would be at Long Bia and in a proper house.

Early the next morning Buwan came again.

"Tuan, we are afraid to go on."

"Why did you promise you would go if I got the third *prau* then?" Herman asked impatiently. "You even suggested the plan and now you won't go."

A compromise was reached. We would all eat lunch and then take off. About 2 o'clock we finally got away. By then the river had begun to go down. Herman and I led in the first *prau*. There were still rapids and whirlpools. However, we were so glad to be on our way that I forgot to tighten up. I was saving that until we came to a place near Long Bia that Herman said was "bad." There, according to him, we would pass through a narrow place with high boulders on both sides.

Time after time the paddlers stood to pilot us around the edge of a whirlpool or through a rapid. One place seemed worse than anything we had seen that day. Herman kept telling me, "These are bad, but none of them are really dangerous until just before we come to Long Bia."

After passing a series of "bad and long" rapids, one of the men turned to us and said, "Now we are free." We didn't understand—we hadn't gone through that narrow gorge Herman had been telling me about. Herman, too, looked bewildered. Then we realized what had happened. The water had been so high we had literally passed right over those huge boulders.

We truly were free! Glorious feeling!

Long Bia was not empty. Dorothy Van Patter and her girls were there. They were surprised that we had come on such a "high-water" day.

I could have hugged her when she said, "How about a drink of ice water and perhaps a dish of ice cream?"

Ice water and a dish of ice cream? It was our first in more than a year. Never in this world had there been such good ice water and such good ice cream! That evening, after John arrived from Tandjong Selor, we ate a delicious dinner, complete with silverware, dishes and glassware. And that night we slept on real, honest-to-goodness beds. John had brought our first-class mail up from Tandjong Selor. We talked and read letters, ate ice cream and drank ice water and talked some more. What more could two bone-weary missionaries want?

Before retiring I took a bath, and for the first time since leaving home I took off my clothes. I was shocked to see how much weight I had lost. Not until then did I understand the statement: "Nyonya, how thin you are!" I was thin, all right, but the world was a good place again. We really did have friends. They still loved us. The letters proved it—all 165 of them.

Eventually we arrived in Makassar for the conference. We both had scurvy and the insides of our mouths were like raw steak. Although I had been asked to be conference hostess, they took one look at me and excused me from the responsibility.

How incredibly wonderful was the conference! Because of our long isolation we valued the fellowship of the other missionaries more than ever. Did the others notice how we came early to the sessions and stayed late? We were starving for a chance to associate with people of our own race and to talk "American."

17

The Final Chapter

The preceding chapters (except for certain inserted sections) have been written by Mary Thornhill Dixon, my wife. It has become necessary for me, Herman Dixon, to finish the story. Let me explain.

While we were at conference, April 8 through 24, in Benteng Tinggi, war broke out between the Indonesian soldiers serving in the Dutch army and the Indonesian guerrillas who were fighting the Dutch for their independence. Four hundred houses were destroyed and many hundreds of people were killed in nearby Makassar.

It is a wonder that any of our missionaries escaped unscathed as the fighting raged for five days and nights around the Mission. The buildings were struck repeatedly by shells. Three whizzed by Mary's face. One night, with a fire from the village blazing toward the Mission headquarters, the missionaries went to prayer. A few minutes later a wind arose from the other direction. The fire receded.

Another day the battle approached the Mission. The defending soldiers began to set up machine guns around the perimeter of the compound. Again the missionaries went to prayer. After about an hour, there was no more firing. The battle had gone the other way.

No decision of conference brought so much rejoicing to us as the appointment of Bud and Ruth Rudes to the Apo Kayan. We had prayed earnestly that God would send the couple of His choosing to join us in the completion of the missionary task.

We met with the Rudes at conference to plan our schedule for the year. When we were finished, there was a list of things 10 couples would not have been able to do. However, we decided to roll up our sleeves and set to work to accomplish as much as possible before our furlough the following year.

The plan was to quickly bring the Rudes, ourselves and a supply of food to Long Nawang. However, nothing moves quickly in Borneo—and frequently not at all—as in the case of the Rudes' coming. After some food had been flown in from Data Dian, we discovered a gasoline shortage. There was barely enough fuel for one more trip, and there would be no more until it came from Makassar. Since we had already been away from home six months, it was agreed that we should head for Long Nawang and the Rudes would follow as soon as possible.

It was a joy to introduce them to missionary life and work in the Apo Kayan when they finally arrived. Their coming brightened our home and lightened our work load.

We learned that while we were away at conference three more churches had become self-supporting and the half-finished workers' house at Long Nawang had been completed. Also two church-owned *praus* had been made so the pastors could freely travel the district. At one village the chief and two-thirds of the 1,600 population had turned to Christ. One of our first tasks after our return was to help them destroy their fetishes.

In addition, Amat, one of the most influential of King Lendjau's family, had come to the Lord and a number of remarkable healings had taken place. The bad news was that the *Bungan Malan* religion now had 12,000 followers.

At Long Nawang, people were coming to Christ in unprecedented numbers. After one Sunday morning service, 12 professed Christ and immediately went to their homes to destroy their idols. Another time, at the close of an afternoon service, five Christians came forward to repent of their sinful lives. Churches were being organized, Sunday schools established, training conferences held for native evangelists. The future looked bright. God was at work in the Apo Kayan. The harvest was ripe.

Then tragedy struck.

THE FINAL CHAPTER

In February Mary suddenly became very weak, lost her appetite and dropped five pounds within one week. Just as she seemed to rally, an influenza epidemic swept through the area. We could not tell that there was anything seriously wrong except for extreme weakness. I committed her to the Lord and she seemed to recover.

Then, in April, we noticed a large swelling on the left side of her abdomen. It gradually spread to her whole stomach. There were periods of extreme, throbbing pain and acute indigestion. She could hardly eat. We knew we should take her to the coast for medical care as soon as possible, but she was not able to make the journey over the rapids. The previous trip had nearly cost her her life.

We tried to send a wire to Al Lewis down on the coast requesting the plane to come in. But the antique wireless was out of commission.

We sent a letter downriver by canoe. We waited and hoped and prayed. Meanwhile, it seemed that we could see the tumor growing bigger every day. The darkness was crowding in around us. The heavens seemed to be a brass sounding board deflecting our prayers and sending them back to us.

During those weeks, some students came upstream from the Long Bia Bible School. We asked why the plane had not been bringing us supplies every month.

"Why, haven't you heard?" the students replied. "The big, new plane was wrecked on a takeoff. It is badly damaged. It will be months before it can be repaired."

That news seemed to be Mary's death knell. Perhaps another missionary grave would be added to those in the valley behind our house. We waited and we prayed.

Time passed until July 5. On that memorable date we were sitting on the front porch of the house when we heard the sound of an airplane coming up the river. *How could it be? The Mission plane was wrecked and no other plane ever came to this remote part of Borneo over the mountains and beyond the rapids.*

The plane circled around the village three times, gradually descending with each pass. Then eight bags without parachutes were pushed out over the field in back of our house. It was the first mail we had received all year.

There was a note from Al Lewis down at the coast explaining that the plane that had dropped the bags was chartered from the Dutch Shell Oil Company and that in three days it would come again to the landing at Data Dian—the only place in the district where it was possible for a plane to land—in order to fly Mary out to a doctor. What a relief! God had heard our prayers!

What a busy time we had getting ready! Only one day to do all of our packing and one to go downstream to Data Dian by *prau*. We took the first-class mail with us and left the magazines and second-class mail. And we turned our food supplies over to the Rudes who would remain in the Apo Kayan.

Although we arrived at Data Dian on the appointed day, the plane did not come on the third day as promised. In fact, it was seven days before it put in its appearance bright and early one morning. Then, flying very high over the mountains, it passed by. *Could it be that after this wait, the plane could not land?*

It was more than Mary could take. She retreated into the little house where we were staying and sat on the edge of her folding cot, not knowing whether to pray or cry.

An hour passed.

Then one of the Dyak schoolboys shouted, "The foreign bird is returning!" The plane circled once, dropped down over the mountain and landed at the sandbar in front of the village. Out stepped two strange Dutchmen who had never made that difficult and dangerous landing before.

"We have come to fly Mrs. Dixon to the doctor," the pilot announced.

And fly us they did! Instead of taking off the way Al Lewis usually did, by following the river, the pilot stood the plane on its tail in the water and took off up the side of the mountain!

An hour and a half later we landed on the island of Tarakan where Dutch Shell had a large oil refinery. A big, black limousine was awaiting our arrival, and Mary was rushed to the company hospital.

The doctor examined her. Then, turning to me, he said, "I'm sorry, but it is too late. I can only tell you that it is one of 40 different kinds of tumors. If you want to save your wife's life, get her to a specialist right away."

"Can we go home by boat?" I inquired.

"No," replied the doctor, "she will die on the way. You must go by air. Already it is too late."

Ten days from the time we were flown out of the interior of Borneo we arrived at the San Francisco airport. We had spent three-and-a-half days in four different planes.

We stepped down from the plane to the greetings of Mary's twin brother and sister, her aged father, two other brothers and a sister-in-law from Ohio. The relatives from Ohio just "happened" to be in California. It was a wonderful reunion.

The day following our arrival back in the States we were told, "There is no better hospital anywhere than the University of California Hospital in San Francisco. All the staff members are specialists." But there was one problem—a patient had to be recommended by a family physician to be admitted and, even then, a vacancy might not occur for weeks.

About 3 o'clock on Sunday afternoon, Mary's youngest brother, a dental surgeon who had come out from Ohio, called the hospital.

"This is Dr. Thornhill speaking," he said. "My sister has just arrived from Borneo and is seriously ill with a tumor. It is an emergency. Can you receive her?"

The voice on the other end replied, "I am Dr. Groves. There happens to be a one-bed vacancy. If you will bring her here within an hour, I will receive her myself."

The tumor proved to be unusual with numerous characteristics which puzzled even the specialists. After many experiments, two operations, several blood transfusions and a series of X-ray treatments, she was finally discharged—"cured."

In March of 1952 I drove Mary to Cleveland where she took the usual physical examination required for all returning missionaries. The doctors found that she had an infected kidney, an enlarged spleen—probably caused by previous attacks of malaria—and her blood count was precariously low.

One of the doctors asked Mary if she planned to go back to Borneo. When she replied in the affirmative, he said, "Well, not for a year or two anyway."

In April, another tumor appeared in the glands on the left side of Mary's neck. But it didn't slow her down. She continued to take speaking engagements.

A year later, on April 2, 1953, at sunrise, Mary passed away. A week before she had told a friend that she wanted to spend Easter in heaven. Her wish was granted. What a joyous Easter it must have been for her!

We took her body back to Warren, Ohio, for burial in the family cemetery lot. There, in The Christian and Missionary Alliance Church, in keeping with her wishes, a simple but beautiful memorial service was held. The gospel was preached, exalting Mary's Lord. Her favorite hymn, "Great Is Thy Faithfulness," was sung.

Thousands of friends all over the world who knew Mary and loved her would agree that Dr. Harry M. Shuman's text was not only appropriate for the funeral but applicable to her life: "Blessed are the dead which die in the Lord from henceforth: Yea, saith the Spirit, that they may rest from their labours; and their works do follow them" (Revelation 14:13b KJV).

Today, she stands among the great cloud of witnesses, urging us on to a final, glorious victory.

Epilogue

After Mary's death, Bill, her brother, went to tell Georgie Minter, the missionary aunt who had returned from China to look after the motherless Thornhill children, that Mary had died.

When Bill walked into the room, Georgie said, "Mary is gone." She went on to explain that she had wrestled with God, asking Him to take her life instead of Mary's. The Lord, however, told her that her work was not complete.

In early 1954, Herman wrote the Mission:

> After months of prayerful deliberation I have come to the conclusion that it is not God's will for me to return to the mission field, but that God would call me into some other avenue of Christian service. Therefore, it is with a feeling of deep regret that I tender my resignation as an active missionary of The Christian and Missionary Alliance after some 20 years of service in Borneo.

Herman passed away on March 23, 1994, in St. Petersburg, Florida.